Through Ancient Gates

Through Ancient Gates

Reliving Norwich History:
our medieval city defences
recreated in words and
and drawings by

Leo R. Jary

Published by the Larks Press

Ordnance Farmhouse
Guist Bottom, Dereham NR20 5PF

01328 829207

Larks.Press@btinternet.com
Website: www.booksatlarkspress.co.uk

British Library Cataloguing-in-Publication Data
A catalogue record for this book is available
from the British Library

ISBN 978 1 904006 59 6

To Femke and Kate

Contents

FOREWORD by DEREK JAMES

*'On Monday last the ruthless hands of men began to execute
the sentence of demolition passed upon the venerable gates of this city:
Brazen Doors have met their fate, St Stephen's follows next.'*

So wrote the editor of the Norfolk Chronicle on October 27 1792 when work got underway to destroy the magnificent gates which had protected the proud city of Norwich through turbulent times.

But in Norwich of the time many people couldn't see the point of paying taxes to maintain the gates, walls and ditches which surrounded them; they had, it was claimed, become a costly nuisance. It was time for them to go.

While other ancient cities decided it would be good to keep some of the structures for future generations, in Norwich they were soon disappearing in clouds of dust. In years to come more evidence of the gates and the impressive walls which had surrounded Norwich for so long came tumbling down in the name of progress – to make way for roads.

Today we have ring roads instead of walls and gates.

Dotted around, sections of the walled city, fragments of a distant time, still stand, but rampant civic vandalism, aided and abetted by the Luftwaffe in the second World War, destroyed most of it.

And as for the gates... we can only imagine what they must have looked like, guarding the second most important city in all of medieval England.

That is until now.

Thanks to Leo R. Jary we can now step back in time and see them in all their glory – towering over 21st century Norwich.

This is a local history book with a difference. The author has combined ancient and modern and has come up with a publication different from any others.

Not only is he a fine writer he is also an accomplished artist and he has put his skills to good use in this wonderful book.

His exquisite drawings and words bring history alive.

Each gate has a story of its own and we discover the part it played in the life of the city.

Turn a page and see what Norwich looked like when the city was enclosed by the most extensive defences in the land – the longest walls and the most gates and towers, enclosing more acres of land than London.

Congratulate Leo R. Jary for coming up with a marvellous book which will appeal to people of all ages, interested in the rich and colourful history of Norwich – locals and visitors.

So take your copy and go exploring. Head north, south, east and west and imagine a time when the gates stood high and mighty – protecting the fine city and its people.

Step Through Ancient Gates...

Derek James

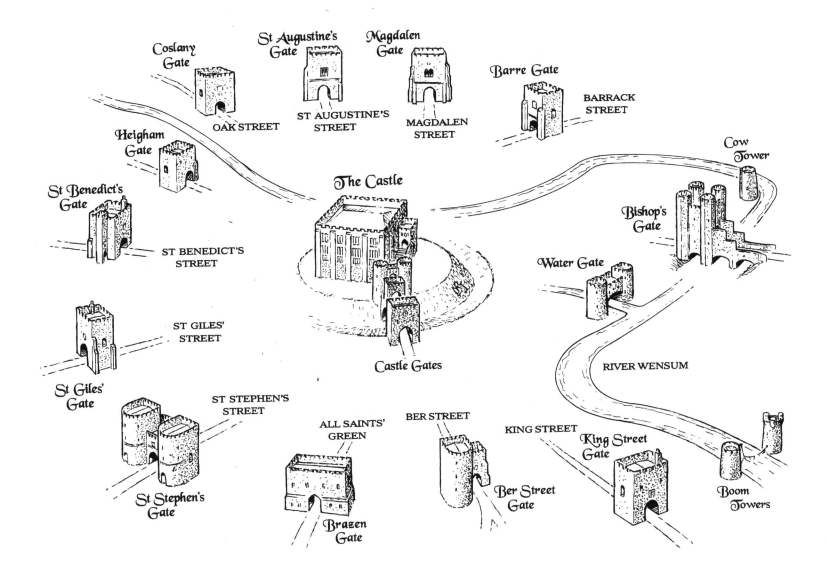

Coslany
Gate

St Augustine's
Gate

Magdalen
Gate

Barre Gate

BARRACK
STREET

OAK STREET

ST AUGUSTINE'S
STREET

MAGDALEN
STREET

Cow
Tower

Heigham
Gate

The Castle

Bishop's
Gate

St Benedict's
Gate

Water Gate

ST BENEDICT'S
STREET

ST GILES'
STREET

Castle Gates

RIVER WENSUM

St Giles'
Gate

ST STEPHEN'S
STREET

ALL SAINTS'
GREEN

BER STREET

KING STREET

King Street
Gate

St Stephen's
Gate

Ber Street
Gate

Boom
Towers

Brazen
Gate

Preface

We Norwich folk live in a fine historic city- we have a noble Norman Cathedral, a commanding castle, an exceptional number of churches, and streets lined with houses full of ancient secrets. They were built with the finest stone from Normandy and from our own English hills, with flints from quarries on Mousehold, and from the rough red bricks kilned here for hundreds of years. But for all that, we do have cause to envy places like York, Lincoln and all those other cities and towns that still have their ancient gates. Here we are in Norwich, the second most important city in medieval England, having then the most extensive city defences, the longest sweeps of wall, the most city gates and towers, all enclosing more acres of land than London itself. Of all those ancient defences, we now have only some stretches of ruined wall and stubs of towers. There are two almost whole towers, but no gates.

It is highly unlikely that any of our ancient gates could ever be rebuilt, but there is no harm in imagining how this modern city would look if we still had them. So here they are, rebuilt in lines, textures and words, set against our present day streets. I have shown all the gates as they were before 1720; they were so much closer to their original state then. Later in that same century they were 'tidied-up' and lost a great deal of their character.

Please allow me some artistic licence though, because at least two feet at the bottom of each gate would by now be hidden below the present road surface. In fact, some foundations must still be there.

But what if those ancient gates had survived? While most of them had archways wide enough for some modern vehicles to pass through, in reality the roads, the flow of modern traffic and even some buildings would have evolved quite differently. With a few exceptions, I have limited the history of the associated streets to the time when the gates were still standing.

I offer no apology for removing the street furniture, the lamps, lights and signs, the ugly necessities that spoil such views, or for measuring the gates in yards and feet, as they did in those final years.

You may want to carry this book with you, and stand where I made my sketches. In adjacent streets you will find signs of people, places and events that were close to the gates in their time; in St Benedict's and St Giles' for example, look among the paving slabs for the decorative panels by Norwich Heart, and everywhere for the blue plaques recording famous people. There is much to see in this fine old city. But first, to our ancient gates...

Leo R. Jary, Norwich 2011.

Gatehouse, Wall and Arcades

The Walls.

A. **Arcade:** an arched recess, or a series of arches along a length of wall.

T. **Mural Towers:** built at intervals along a city wall, usually projecting forward of it.

B. **Barbican:** outer defence of a castle or gate; confining walls beside the gate approaches.

W. **Alure:** walkway behind a parapet. Shown here with a stone deck and back rails, similar in principle to reconstructed European examples, as in Harderwijk and Zwolle, in the Netherlands.

P. **Pomoerium:** passage way parallel to the city wall, kept clear for urgent action. In Norwich, 'The way under the wall.'

The Battlements

E. **Embrasure** or **crenel:** opening between merlons. Two to three feet wide.

M. **Merlon:** a block of masonry, highest parts of a parapet, enabling soldiers to fire from protected positions. Up to five feet wide, three or more feet high.

L. **Loop:** stone block with an arrow-slit three to four inches wide, three or more feet high. Some were **cross-loops.**

The Walled City

The Norman conquerors first built well placed defensible castles to assert their dominance over the vanquished Saxons. A magnificent cathedral followed. In Norwich they needed to defend this new mile-wide city with embankments and palisades. It was a very open city, with broad meadows and grazing land within the walls, as in Chapelfield and Bull Close. The work of building defences along the two and a half miles of city boundary was a daunting but necessary task.

King Street, Ber Street, Heigham and St Augustine's gates are recorded earlier, but by 1270 these timber structures had begun to be replaced with walls of the local building stone, flint. They quarried it from hurriedly opened pits in the lower slopes of Mousehold Heath, and from the ancient and derelict Romano-British town at Caistor Saint Edmund's two and a half miles to the south. From there by the cart load they hauled the hard grey flint nodules from its ruined walls to Norwich. To cover the cost, there was imposed in 1294 a programme of taxation that lasted for twenty-five years. By 1319 the work was nearly finished and the city was defended with stone gates and over two miles of high walls. They were completed by a local benefactor, the successful and wealthy merchant Richard Spynk, who took it upon himself in 1342 to provide a high proportion of the cost of the city defences. He paid for the completion of gates, mural towers, some lengths of wall and almost all the weapons to arm them. The weapons, mostly installed on the fighting tops of the gates and towers, were mainly stone-throwing devices*: thirty *espringalls* (springolds or springaulds, a type of catapult), four *arblasters*, (a sort of crossbow) and one hundred stone balls for each weapon.

Work on the defences had been sporadic and stretched over a period of seventy years. Nonetheless completion of the gates was timely. In the 1380s there was the threat of French invasions, and Norwich citizens noted with alarm the bitter experience of Southampton, which suffered sea-borne attacks in 1383. It was recorded that *'All trade ceased for a year.'*

Many of the gates were built to a height of thirty-six feet and width of twenty-one feet, and most were fairly square in plan. Many of the archways were only twelve feet high, and eight feet wide. These buildings were small compared to the wall gates of other cities. They began with solid foundations and walls with inner and outer faces. The space between the faces was then filled with mortar and rubble, following the practice of the Romans. The method can be seen in the surviving sections of our city walls. The basic methods and tools used by medieval builders had changed little since the time of their Roman forebears, and builders of our time would know how to work alongside these medieval craftsmen, even without their power tools. Power in those days was in the muscles of many men. There was a large workforce of stone masons, carpenters, blacksmiths, mortar mixers, lead-workers and general labourers. All loads were moved and lifted by the use of strong ropes, pulleys, winches and simple cranes. From decorated panels and illuminated documents by contemporary artists* we have informative drawings of construction scenes, with the architects, craftsmen and labourers at various stages of their work; we see their tools and apparatus, and even the accidents that often befell the men. Nowadays, health and safety regulators would quite properly forbid the use of their methods, machinery and scaffolding. Basic scaffolding consisted of a timber framework built up from the ground, braced or cross-braced and rope-bound. Its stability, when heavily loaded, depended upon the strength and binding of the rope lashings that held it all together.

* See illustrations, page 27

* See References, page 71; 'Medieval Building Techniques.'

At lower levels, men worked from planks resting on trestles; for work at higher levels, on such as the Cow Tower, 'flying scaffolds' were used. For these, planks were supported on timbers projecting through previously built masonry. Timbers were removed and reused as the work progressed upward.

Cranes, with their booms, windlass drums and winch wheels, were built or modified for each building site. They were held firmly in place by weights on their wooden cross-feet, and steadied with guy ropes; they were capable of delivering loads to a height of thirty feet. They were not easily repositioned while operating, and could rarely be 'slewed' (horizontally rotated*) for the precise placing of a load, so were regularly dismantled and repositioned. At the appropriate stage, a crane was reassembled in the room above the arch, where it was used to hoist materials for building the walls up to the fighting top level, for placing timbers on the roof and fighting top, and to raise the relatively small amounts of material for constructing the merlons and embrasures.

The crane windlass was worked by a hand-wheel with four or more radial spokes. From its winding drum a strong rope was hauled or eased through pulley blocks, down to the workload. Large loads were grappled by a *'Lewis'*, a pair of scissor-like claws. Simple hooks were used for smaller loads, such as wooden buckets of lime-and-sand mortar, or pallets of flints. Little is known about the braking methods used to prevent loads running out of control, but 'belaying pins' *(kevels)* may have been used against the windlass spokes.**

As the gate illustrations show, there were very narrow corner ashlars *(quoins)* in the main body of the gatehouse and at the slab-like sides of the merlons. Being relatively small, these and the blocks of arrow-slit loops did not demand so much power from the cranes. Some larger and heavier blocks of stone were used in the buttresses, steps and lintels.

* There were slewing cranes in Europe as early as 1340
** See illustrations, page 17

When more lifting power was needed, two-man treadwheel cranes provided it. Our legs are the more powerful of our limbs, and by 'walking' in a big enough diameter wheel, a lot of power can be delivered. Manuscripts held in monastic libraries provided medieval planners with the details of Roman *Magna Rola* treadwheels; it may be that the reading of such documents prompted the reappearance of treadwheels in early medieval England and Europe. There are surviving treadwheel cranes at Guildford in Surrey (a scheduled ancient monument), and at Harwich in Essex (a grade II listed building), both dating from the late 1600s. Reconstructions of treadwheel cranes can be seen at Treigny in France (for a castle rebuilding project), at Bruge in Belgium, and at the 'Medieval Fortress' in Leadhill, Arkansas. Results of these experiments suggest that a four or five yard diameter two-man treadwheel could lift three tons at a time. It is doubtful, however whether so much power was needed to raise materials for the building of our city gates, walls or towers.

Large timbers and masonry were worked on at ground level; small-work was done on portable benches, placed anywhere convenient, sometimes high up in the gatehouse. Fired materials, such as bricks and tiles were made off-site. All workable materials were cut with hand tools. Most of their chisels, mallets, awls and hammers, we would recognise, but some of their axes had very broad blades that looked like the heads of pikes or halberds. Wood that needed well finished surfaces, was mostly 'dressed' (surfaces smoothed) with an adze; these were axe-like but with blades turned sideways. Adze blades were of various lengths and widths.

Carpenters used a variety of other cutting tools. Their bow saws and frame saws looked rather like hacksaws. There were double-ended two-man saws for big timbers; some of these were fitted with side bearers for guiding the blade along the required saw-line.

Mallets and wedges were used for splitting lengths of timber.

An enormous amount of wood was used on medieval building sites. Apart from the forest of scaffolding poles, working platforms and plank walkways, there were stout timbers for floor beams and the temporary framework for arches and other openings in the masonry. Wheelbarrows, handcarts, hods, sledges, buckets, panniers and ladders were all made of wood and had to be replaced from time to time.

These building sites were full of noise, accumulated from the clap of timbers being piled up, the sawing and hammering of the carpenters, orders shouted to men on scaffolding, the creaking and groaning of cranes at work, and the hammering of the blacksmiths at their forges, shaping tools, locks, hinges and nails. (Some of these may have been supplied by local metal workers.)

Supporting walls for both sides of the archway grew with the other walls up to the 'spring,' the point at which the arch masonry would start to curve. Scaffolding was then erected in the open space of the proposed arch, and over that was assembled a wooden former or template, which dictated the shape and size of the arch. Shaped stones, *voussoirs,* were then 'formed' around the template, a practice well known today. Almost all our city gate arches were pointed, with an all important keystone at the centre. Few keystones were distinguishable by their size or shape.

Arches naturally push outward, so it was as well to have wide walls at each side to stabilise the great mass of stone above it. We can see by the proportions of our gates that this principle was well applied to most of them. As more masonry was built up above the arches and other walls, pairs of strong oak doors,* or sometimes a single door, were built toward the city end of each gate arch. A portcullis was built into the other end, of a size to fit the freestone running groves in the arch masonry. The portcullis was most often a simple lattice of iron or strong timber. Some had horizontal cross bars of

* See illustrations, page 20

timber pierced vertically with metal rods. Many of the components were prepared off-site.*

Each of the city gates had a room above the archway occupied by a gatekeeper, who in pre-Reformation times, was often a hermit. The room was also used as a prison cell.

It was the keeper's duty to watch over the gate and the attached lengths of city wall. From this room a small door allowed access to the *alure* (wall walkway). These hermit rooms** were not at all luxurious, as they also served as a shelter for guards on wall duty, and had to accommodate the windlass for winding up the portcullis. The windlass may have been adapted from parts of a crane left intentionally in the hermit room during building.

Climatic changes prompted important alterations to the hermit rooms. In the 1200s and 1300s there were frequent storms, high rainfall and mild winters – all indications of a warmer climate. One hundred years later, by which time all the gates had been built, it was even warmer, so the upper-floor galleries of inns and many grand houses, were open for most of the year. After another one hundred years, in Elizabethan times, the climate was colder, and those same inns enclosed their galleries. It may have been then that the first fireplaces were added to some hermit rooms, but with fully functioning chimney stacks being added rather later.

The city officers who first planned the medieval defences did not intend to build the gates bigger than military or commercial needs demanded; with small arches, it was easier to control traffic through the gates, and easier to hold them against enemy attack.

The small archways were adequate for a few hundred years, and no one could have foreseen a time when bigger vehicles would be carrying heavier loads. When that time came, it was found helpful to protect the bottom corners of the archways with stone 'legs' set at such an angle that cartwheels were deflected away from the masonry.

* See illustrations, page 19
** For convenience, referred to as such throughout this book.

13

We would know so much less about the city gates and walls if it were not for the work of three observant men. From John Kirkpatrick's book of 1711, *A Walk Round Norwich Walls,* from Henry Ninham's, *Ancient City Gates of Norwich* of 1720, and the engravings and drawings made by his son, John Ninham, in 1792 and 1793, we have inherited a wealth of images of enormous historic value.

The height of the walls was generally twenty-four feet, higher than most houses, and high enough, added to the depth of the city ditch, to deter attack with scaling ladders. Surviving fragments of wall are very informative. The thickness was almost six feet, made up of two leaves: an inner leaf of at least three feet, in which arched recesses *(arcades)* were formed during building, and an outer leaf of about two feet. The outer leaf fully closed the walls, but allowed arrow slits *(loops)* to be placed at the centre of each arcade. The two leaves are apparent in the wall at the St Stephen's end of Chapelfield Road. At Barn Road, near St Benedict's gate, the walls now have fully open arcades where almost all the outer leaf has been lost. Other almost complete arcades are up to eight feet high and seven feet wide. There are fine examples in a length of wall adjoining the Black Tower in Bracondale, in the most southerly part of the city.

City Defences were made more effective by having towers *(murals)* spaced along the lengths of city wall. These towers varied in height from twenty-seven to thirty or more feet. Well preserved examples are the Octagonal Tower at the junction of Silver and Bull Close Roads, and the Black Tower in Bracondale. There were more than thirty murals, many placed at bends in the wall where there would otherwise be blind spots. From the sides of these towers, defenders could *'enfilade'* i.e. shoot arrows along the outer face of the wall. The trend in the 1300s was to build the towers circular in section, half inside, half outside the wall. Some were half circles projecting entirely to the outside.

Most circular towers had interior stone stairs up to the alures; simple ladders may have been used in the half-circle towers. There were at least two rectangular towers: one close to St Augustine's Gate, and another between Ber Street Gate and Brazen Gate, long known as the Broad Tower. The greater part of their mass projected out from the city wall. It is possible that Brazen Gate was first built as another of these rectangular mural towers; that would explain its unusual shape and the fact that it was not separately listed as a gate in the mural report of 1345.*

At the close of the Ice Age, water from the melting glaciers cut a broad river valley through our city area, where now flows the Wensum. The presence of this river made it necessary to build the wall in two long sweeping arcs: one well to the south and west of the river, and another, shorter arc to the north of it. The marshy banks of the river marked much of the eastern boundary of the city and were a practical part of the defences, as did the shorter, otherwise undefended length between Heigham and Coslany Gates.

As can be seen on the contour map (page 70), the river is a 'meander.' One of the characteristics of meanders is that they change their flow often; as older channels silt up, the water finds other places to flow, and new channels are cut. Such changes to the river flow occurred throughout the lifetime of the city gates. In the New Mills and Coslany Bridge area, the river had at one time divided into channels with three islands, at other times two islands, or one large island. In that part of the river closest to the last mural tower on the north wall at Coslany Gate, there was one big island. Now there is only a single channel right through the city. The depth and width of the river was changeable too, but records show that it was usually navigable for shallow-draught barges and fishing boats, but rarely suitable for seagoing ships; so different to the wider and deeper rivers known to the Romans of 200 A.D., when the

---

* See 'Battlements', page 21.

Wensum, Yare and Tas, were used by their seagoing merchant ships.

Meltwater from the last fragments of the glaciers also cut streams which fed the River Wensum. Thousands of years later, what remained of the streams were known as *cockeys.** Only in relatively modern times has the city lost sight of them. Pools or pits had formed mid-way of their flows which became the last visible remnants of their presence. 'Jack's Pit' was at the junction of Surrey Street and All Saints' Green, in a stretch of the Great Cockey; the 'Muspole' was at the junction of Muspole Street and Colegate; the pit of Pit Lane was at the opening of what became Rigby's Court; and there was another in Pitt Street (later given that extra 't', it is said, to honour the Prime Minister William Pitt the Younger). Foul by sight and smell, all were filled-in. No doubt there were others, long lost even to folk memory.

For most of the years of the city gates, there were five river crossings, including Bishop's Bridge, which is the only original medieval city bridge surviving. The others are rebuilds. Up-river to the west is the Whitefriars' Bridge, rebuilt several times, always in wood until the most recent replacement. It may have been the first of all the bridges, being an important link between the Benedictine Cathedral Priory and the monastery of the Whitefriars. It was once thought that the first Fye Bridge was the oldest, but according to Blomefield, 'Fye' meant five, it being, he believed, the fifth river crossing to be built. St George's was quite early and often rebuilt, but always in timber until the Portland stone version of 1784 was erected. Coslany Bridge marks a very old crossing, dating back to a time of two river channels, with one bridge over each of them. The first Coslany Bridge in stone was finished in 1521, just one year before the city gates were made ready for a feared invasion by the French. It would have been no surprise to the people of those days to find, to their dismay, that enemy forces had sailed barges all the way up river.

* See map, appendix iv, page 70.

It may be that there was some lively folklore about attacks by pirates. Most of the bridges were stone by the time of Kett's 1549 Rebellion, and all relatively new; little wonder that the city authorities took such a jaundiced view of Earl Warwick's wish to demolish them all as part of his defence against the rebels. They allowed the destruction of Whitefriars' Bridge only, then still of wood.

The city ditch was sixty feet wide, and generally followed the line of the city wall. It may have been dug out as early as 1150, with a mound on the city side thrown up at the same time – the first act of preparing the city defences. The sloping sides of the ditch had to be allowed to settle for many years before the walls could safely be built beside it. From the bottom of the ditch, twenty feet deep, to the tops of the walls, these defences were impressive, and would effectively have hindered attackers and their siege engines.

From the variable terrain along the line of the city wall, it is clear that the flow of water along the city ditch, or how it might hold a body of water, could not have been major considerations when digging its course, although water was bound to accumulate in stretches of it.

Beyond the city ditch, a wide margin of land was kept clear of visual obstructions; it was important for defenders to see what was happening out there. It was also important to have a passageway, a *pomoerium,* kept clear on the city side of the wall; in old Norwich, known as 'the way under the wall.' Three hundred years later, large areas of the ditch must have become filled in, otherwise Kett's rebels would not have been able to break through the wall at Bull Close, or Warwick's men to break into the city at Chapelfield. The fact that they were able to do so may indicate some lack of care by the city authorities, or their disregard for the defensive purpose of the ditch. Orders had been issued from time to time for it to be cleaned and cleared of rubbish, but it seems that the work was not well done.

The roads through the gates were linked to the surrounding country by bridges over the city ditch. Some were timber-built and mounted on trestles; others were supported by stone piers and arches. In some earlier views of the bridges over the ditch, we see high walls at their sides *(barbicans)*. In the earliest years, some centre-spans may have been drawbridges, or counterweighted 'tilts' as in some European cities, such as Amsterdam, Rotterdam and Bruges.

By the 1700s, the bridges were becoming redundant, as was the ditch. Keeping the ditch clean and free of rubbish had been a problem for centuries, and the ditch was no longer a practical defence. By the late 1700s, most of it had been back-filled and made level with the surrounding fields and roads. Almost all the Ninham drawings of the 1790s show clear ground in front of the gates.

Soon after the in-filling of the ditches, citizens and council began to adopt the same attitude to the city walls. For centuries civic leaders had been duty bound to keep walls, gates and ditch in good repair, and for that new taxes had often been levied; *murage* for the walls and gates; *fossage* mainly for the ditch. To most citizens of the late 1780s, gates, walls and ditch were not worth the cost or the trouble they caused, even though another war with France was imminent. None of it was an effective defence of the city. It seems there was little to redeem our ancient gates, walls or most of the towers – even some towers that were used as dwellings.

In *Chase's Norwich Directory* of 1783, the editor wrote this fiery condemnation of them all:

> *'If the city gates were totally erased, the air, and prospects (views) to and from the town, would be much improved. When cities were surrounded by walls and gates, the state of the times made such precautions necessary; but now that the system of war is better understood... they become a nuisance...'*

Of course, removing the gates made no difference to the flow of fresh air, and some people at least regretted losing them. On October 27th 1792, the editor of the *Norfolk Chronicle*, holding on to his sense of history, wrote;

> *'On Monday last the ruthless hands of men began to execute the sentence of demolition passed upon the venerable Gates of this City: Brazen Doors have met their fate, St Stephen's follows next.'*

And sadly, so it did. Heaven knows what the 14th century public benefactor, Richard Spynk would have said; he had, after all, contributed so much to the building of the gates and city walls. Other cities and towns achieved a balance of ancient relics surviving beside modern needs, but unlike York and such places, our gates and walls, having stood for five hundred years, were swept away.

However, some of the streets within the old city – Ber Street, St Stephen's, St Giles', St Benedict's, St Augustine's and Magdalen – have buildings tightly packed right up to the gate sites, while the streets and buildings beyond the old city line tend to be more openly spaced – a good indication of where the gates stood. In this way, and by the remaining fragments of walls and towers, our modern city is still outlined by its ancient past.

Windlass and Treadwheel Cranes

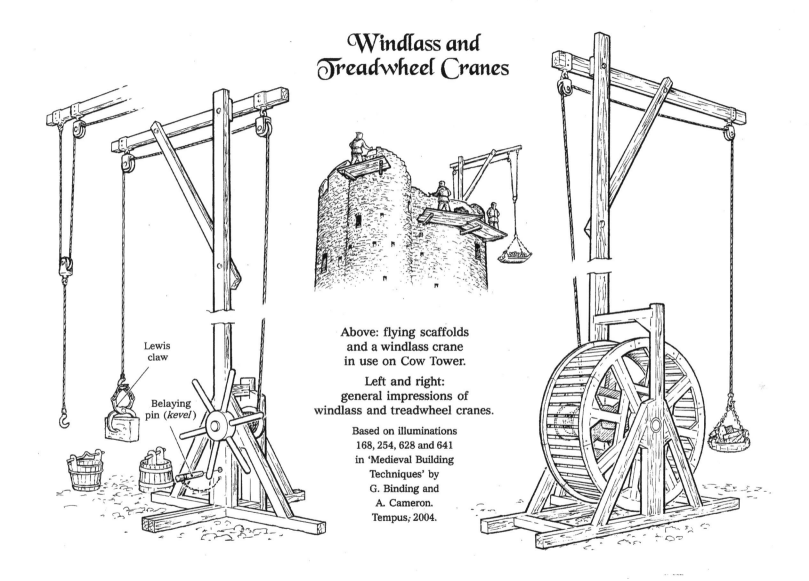

Lewis claw

Belaying pin (*kevel*)

Above: flying scaffolds
and a windlass crane
in use on Cow Tower.

Left and right:
general impressions of
windlass and treadwheel cranes.

Based on illuminations
168, 254, 628 and 641
in 'Medieval Building
Techniques' by
G. Binding and
A. Cameron.
Tempus, 2004.

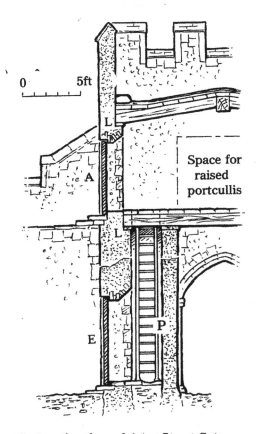

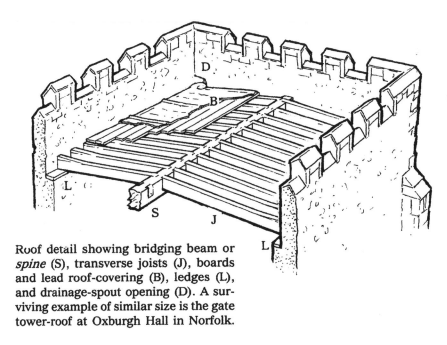

0 ___ 5ft

Space for raised portcullis

Part section through King Street Gate, showing differences of wall thickness, supporting ledges (L), access to alure (A), and gatekeepers entrance (E). The pier (P) had enough width for a ladder to the hermit room

Roof detail showing bridging beam or *spine* (S), transverse joists (J), boards and lead roof-covering (B), ledges (L), and drainage-spout opening (D). A surviving example of similar size is the gate tower-roof at Oxburgh Hall in Norfolk.

Gatehouse Access and Structure

In St Giles' Gate, St Augustine's Gate, and possibly Barre Gate, buttresses also served as stairway turrets. With the out-stand of the turret, the total thickness of pier was up to eight feet, adequate for a four or five-foot diameter winding staircase (*vice*). St Benedict's Gate had an attached stairway turret later enclosed by a southward extension of the gatehouse. Of the four turrets of Bishop's Gate, only two were used as stairways. Heigham, Coslany and Magdalen Gates all had at least one pier wide enough to house a ladder. Ber street, Brazen Gate and St Stephen's all had enough additional structure for each to house a vice. Some gates may have had ground-level access into one of the piers, through a side wall of the archway.

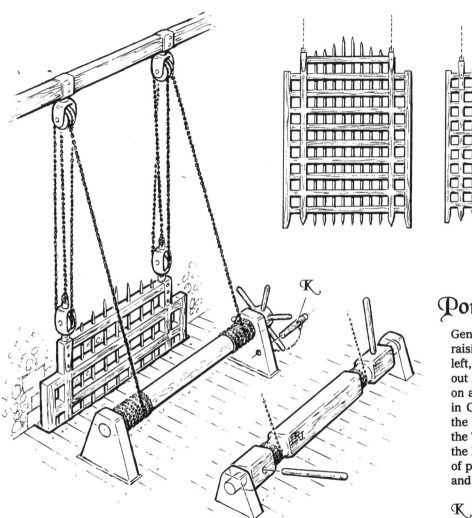

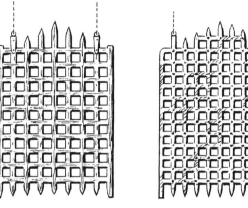

Portcullis and Operating Hoist

General impressions of types of windlass suitable for raising and lowering the portcullis of a city gate. Far left, a type used in castle and city gatehouses throughout Europe. To the immediate left, winding gear based on a surviving working 'barring hoist' at Cahir Castle in County Tipperary, Eire. Hever Castle in Kent has the oldest working original portcullis. Others are at the Tower of London, Amberley Castle in Kent, and at the Monk Bar in York. Above, left to right, three styles of portcullis: wood frame with iron rods, wood lattice and iron lattice.

𝕶 Belaying Pin (*kevel*)

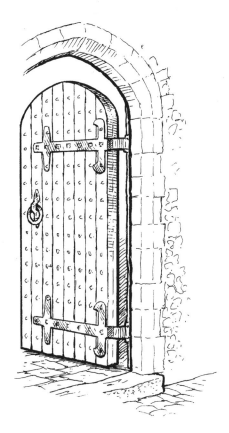

Most city gates had square doors topped with spikes. The top was a little higher than the springing of the arch.

Gatekeeper's door into pier.

One of a pair of doors *(valves)*. This type of arched door may have been used in some gates.

Gatehouse Doors and Wickets

The *'wickets'* or *'clicket-gates'* (shaded) in the lower left of the doors, were for the use of gatekeepers when ordered to keep the main doors of the gates closed. The *'clicket'* was a simple latch, quite like the latch of a garden gate.

⊕ Battlements

In a report of 1345, the numbers of 'battlements' (*Merlons*) on the gates, towers and two arcs of wall were listed.

On the 1 mile of northern arc:

Wall to Coslany Gate –   12;   Gate, 10.
Wall to St Austine's Gate – 69;   Gate, 12.
Wall to Magdalen Gate –   153;   Gate, 13.
Wall to Barre Gate –   178;   Gate, 10.
Wall to riverside tower –   40.
Cow or Meadow Tower –   12.
Bishop's Gate Tower –   38.

On the 1.5 miles of southwest arc:

Boom Towers and wall to
   King Street Gate –   38;   Gate, 14.
Wall to Ber Street Gate–   15;   Gate, 27.
Wall to St Stephen's Gate 307;   Gate, 38.
Wall to St Giles' Gate –   229;   Gate, 15.
Wall to Heigham Gate –   79;   Gate, 4.
Wall to riverside tower –   16.

Appointed wardens arranged for the upkeep and repair of walls, towers and gates, the extent of their responsibilities depending upon the numbers of battlements in their respective wards; however, the numbers were subject to change after repairs and rebuilding.

The Wards;   **C** Conisford   **M** Mancroft
             W Wymer   **O** Over the water

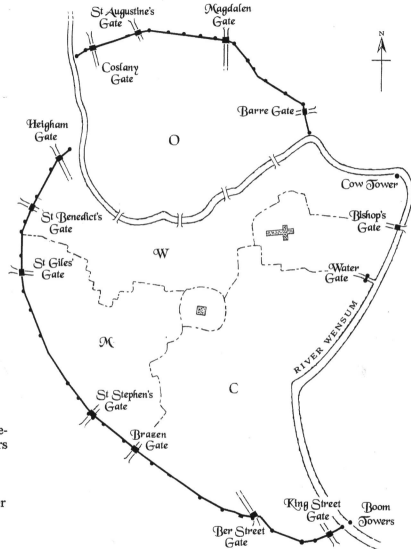

King Street Gate

Buried beneath Norwich City Football Club Stadium is an ancient island of sand and gravel, where some of our earliest settlers left signs of their presence 12,000 years ago. Their river Wensum was braided, and followed a different course from ours today. Millennia passed, bringing us to the final centuries before Christ, when Iron Age people carved tracks across the land. They made some of them through a hilly region destined to become the site of our city of Norwich.

The river must have been important to them, for they made a straight path along its bank, which the Romans later engineered into a marching road. After a few hundred years the Romans withdrew and Saxon pirates, with plunder in mind, found they could sail unhindered up the river, where they beached their longboats and took this same road to other places worth raiding. Some however became settlers who made their homes along this ancient road, and up on the high ridge we now call Ber Street. They built homes, planted crops, and created place names. First, a name for the street: *'Cunegesford'* or *'Konnigsford'* – the King's Ford.

A view of the outer side of the gate. It would have fitted comfortably between the kerbs of the present day King Street. In the distance to the right are new apartments on the corner of Carrow Road; nearby is a piece of the city wall leading down to the riverside Boom Towers. On the left is a 'reconstructed' piece of the city wall, attached to the west wall of the tower, where steps behind a high parapet descended from the hermit room down to the alure (walkway) of the city wall. This wall climbs steeply up to the 'Black Tower' of Bracondale.

The ford so named was where a small stream (a cockey) is thought to have interrupted the road. Their new village, spreading along the road and over the river, they named Carrow. Centuries later the growing city absorbed the village and the street, but the names Carrow and Conesford remain to this day. Sometime before 1175, our first stone gate was built here, marking the most southerly entrance to the city, and the main route to Ipswich, Colchester and London. In about 1200, where there is now Argyle Street, Hildebrand, a mercer, set up a chapel and lodging house for the homeless poor and pilgrims. It served for only a hundred years; but along 'Cunegesford' (now King Street), medieval citizens could pay the friars of the Franciscan and Austin monasteries to pray for their salvation, or offer their own prayers in any of several churches, of which two, both dedicated to St Peter,* were rebuilt in the 1400s by funding from King Street merchants. Some citizens did business with those merchants, whose wharfs lined the riverside. For transporting goods in and out of the city, the merchants paid tolls at the King Street Gate. The river too was a trade-route, so their barges were charged tolls at the nearby Boom Towers.

The great earthquake of Christmas 1480, and another a hundred years later, weakened the King Street Gate, and in due course it was repaired. The gates and towers still had a purpose, although by then it was mainly the collection of tolls. Kett and his adversary the Earl of Warwick would later show the city what gunpowder could do; against such ordnance stone gates and walls were of little use. But the gate survived intact until 1664 when part of it collapsed onto the house of Mr Isaac Wynn. He survived, the gate was repaired, restored again in 1793, then completely demolished in 1794.

* St Peter Permantergate (surviving),
  and St Peter Southgate (a ruin).

23

24

Ber Street Gate

In the view to the left, we are looking across the junction of Queen's Road and Bracondale. Part of the Ber Street Gate pub is visible through the gate arch. The piece of city wall close to the gate is the highest and most complete that we have; it still has the supporting structure of its alure (walkway). The existing low building to the left of the gate closely follows the line of the wall in that direction.

Ber Street Gate stood over the most important road into the city; it was the most direct route to the castle, and was said to be the safest thoroughfare. It follows the top of a commanding ridge.* To the east of the road a steep slope runs down to King Street and the river, and a gentle westward slope to the market and Chapelfield. Because of the importance of this ancient road, Ber Street Gate was one of the earliest built. It was erected, about 1220, as a simple gatehouse, like most of the city gates that followed it. The round tower was probably added to the west side of the gate during the 1300s. In the 1343 accounts of Spynk's work, there is a reference to another, lower tower attached to the east, but later lost. With a tower on each side, it would have looked similar to St Stephen's Gate.

The gate was strategically well placed. Here the wall and the city ditch turned sharply inward, so that an army attacking it had to fight in a corner. In 1549, John Dudley the Earl of Warwick ,would have preferred to enter through this gate, directly on to the tactically important Ber Street Heights, but recognised how well Kett's rebels could defend it. His men had to break through the Brazen Gate instead.

Ber Street Gate was weakened by the 1480 earthquake, and burned by Kett's rebels in 1549. It is probable that the lower tower was too badly damaged in 1549 and not worth rebuilding; the rest of the gate was repaired in 1558. It may have been at this time that the timber bridge and guard rails were replaced with a stone bridge and barbicans. There was further damage from an earthquake in 1580.

In Napoleonic times, the spacious round tower was a commissary for military stores. In 1720 it still had its bridge and barbicans over the city ditch.

* See map, appendix iv, page 70

Ber Street Gate continued

Below: an espringall on the left, and an arblaster, a sort of crossbow, on the right. The diagrams show functions only; these devices were surrounded and supported by much structural framework. Ber Street Gate had six espringalls, more than any other city gate.

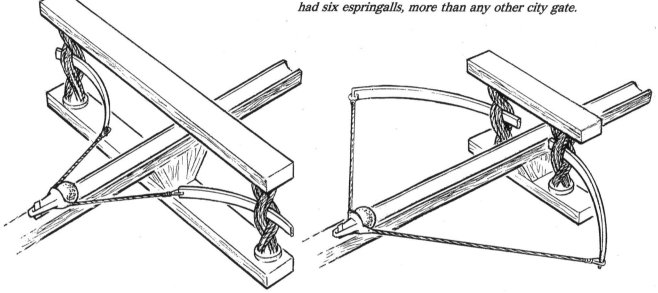

Opposite: a view from a traffic island in Ber Street. The old houses to the left date from the 16th century. Beside the gate is the public house bearing the name 'Ber Strete Gate'. On the right in the foreground is the north-east corner of the church of St John de Sepulchre.

Before 1727, the city side of the gate was probably as plain as other gates; then it was rebuilt in classical style, and the battlements removed. In January 1807, a nearby length of the city wall and a tower collapsed. Some cattle were killed, and no doubt local people feared for their lives. By this time the street had become the local centre for the building trade, and after the gate was taken down in 1808, there was easier access for their teams of horses and heavy wagons loaded with reclaimed building stone – the remains of the demolished gates.

The Brazen Gate

For all their domination, the Norman invaders could not eradicate the Saxon way of life or their language, and Saxon speech and place names persisted. The Saxons had a market on a plain they persistently called *Allderhalen* ('All hallows' – now All Saints' Green) with homes and workshops closely gathered on both sides of it, and they had their own Saxon churches. One of them, St Wynwalloys, gave its name to their widespread parish on land between All Hallows and St Stephen's. At that time the Brazen Gate, built some time before 1285, stood on open land, astride a minor road from the newly finished Norman castle to the nearby hamlets of Lakenham and Harford. By 1300 the population of All Saints' Plain and St Wynwalloy's parish had grown, only to be tragically reduced by the first wave of the Black Death in 1349.

With few surviving people willing or able to tend the worst hit places, churches, houses and fields were left to decay. To get some idea of the scale of this disaster, stand at the junction of All Saints' Green and Surrey Street and look towards St Stephen's; imagine all that land as far as Queen's Road in total desolation. Somewhere there, the church of St Wynwalloy faded away. Perhaps in memory of it, the Brazen Gate was for a time known as 'St Winnold's Gate'; now the name is only recalled by Winall's Yard, off the southern end of All Saints' Green.

A view from the corner of Queen's Road and the minor road named 'Brazen Gate'. The big square building behind and to the left of the gate is the famous Ivory House, built by Thomas Ivory in 1771, twenty-one years before the gate was demolished.

For generations All Saints' Plain had a swine market, so the gate was commonly known as Swine Gate. When the massive wooden door within the archway was reinforced with iron straps, it became known as the 'Iron Door.' Both names were used until 1500, then new buildings filled more of the space between the old Allderhalen and the gate. These were smarter houses for well-to-do citizens, so the pigs were obliged to move out of the city. For thirteen more years the gate was known as the 'Iron Door' until it was remodelled with brass-edged 'posterns' (side gates), and so became known as the Brazen Gate. In 1543, the ditch outside the gate was filled and packed with earth, a causeway to replace the bridge.

With its unusual width, Brazen Gate had the appearance of a miniature fort. When Kett's rebels occupied the city in 1549, they reinforced the gate with massive beams, for they realised that, by its proximity to the tactically important Ber Street Heights, it would be a prime target for royal forces attempting to recapture the city. However, it was not a problem for the Earl of Warwick's artillery. The doors, beams and iron straps were easily shattered by cannon shot.

The gate had six loops (arrow-slits) in its outer face. In the 1700s, some were replaced with windows. In 1726 the council ordered that the arch be made wider *'for a coach or cart to pass through.'* Even after that, for all the great mass of the gate, its archway was little more than eight feet wide. With the new work done, this peculiar portal became known as Newgate; but citizens recalled the brassware used 200 years earlier, so the name 'Brazen Gate' persisted.

The gate was demolished in 1792. Now there are only this busy junction and a minor road to the south that carry the name 'Brazen Gate.'

St Stephen's Gate

This gate marked the end of long journeys from London and other towns to the south-west of Norwich, inluding Cambridge and Bury St Edmunds. It became a ceremonial gate, where Kings and Queens began their royal visits. And yet, in the 1200s, this was a poor district, as its early Saxon name 'Nedeham' tells us; *'a poor hamlet'*. But, like many other streets of the city, St Stephen's was well built-up by the 1500s, and by then this gate had earned its special regard as the grandest entrance, and grand it was, decorated for visiting dignitaries, with colourful banners, shields, flowers, and enlivened with music and fanciful plays.

For anyone else though, merchants, farmers, carriers, people coming to market, this gate was often decorated in a manner that warned them of the terrible punishments that could fall upon any who broke the law here. There were times when severed heads on spikes above the parapets, like macabre heraldic crowns on the shoulders of the gate, watched over the archway, attended by the quartered body parts of 'traitors'. For many generations, that scene was commonplace and it may be that some felt more secure for seeing this cruel proof that civic authority was firmly upheld here. Only a little less sinister were the St Stephen's Gate gallows.

From 1315, there was a leper hospital with a chapel and cottages; in 1469 it became a poor house. It was near the site, in later years, of the Norfolk and Norwich Hospital.

Viewed from the southwest side of Queens Road. To the right, near to the entrance of the Queens Road car park, is a piece of ruined wall and mural tower.

In the beginning of August 1578, Norwich's civic leaders learned that Queen Elizabeth, on her Royal Progress, was already in Suffolk, and would come to Norwich sooner than expected, less than two weeks ahead. St Stephen's Gate was hurriedly repaired, masonry was re-rendered, battlements restored, and a new portcullis was fitted. Of course, there were no heads or torsoes on show, and the gallows were hidden from view. They could do little about the rough country road to the gate, except cover the longest stretch of it from Harford Bridge with fresh gravel. On that road, on Saturday the 16th of August, came the Queen, riding side-saddle at the head of a 'very great traine, eight of the privy councill, diverse noble personages, both lords and ladies, and three French imbassators' (quoted by Blomefield). As she drew near, she heard the cheering crowds and saw the high city walls stretching away to her right and left, and rising up in the middle of her view, the two rounded towers of the grandly decorated St Stephen's Gate. Above the arch were three heraldic shields: the Queen's own arms, the Norwich civic arms and the shield of St George, all between colourful flying banners. Through the arch they went, to more cheers, more decorations, ringing church bells, and music and song by the Norwich Waits, then onward into the city.

The citizens would later regret how much they had spent outdoing each other in furnishings and dress. There were those who chose to look grand sitting astride a horse, even though they had never before owned or needed one, and they certainly didn't need the high cost of keeping it. Before Queen Elizabeth arrived, suitable steeds for ceremonial use had to be sought far from the city.

St Stephen's Gate continued

Poor Norwich; the civic leaders too would learn later the alarming cost of that Royal visit; and for all that, this tough minded Queen probably didn't care how the city officers and citizens looked. But far worse than the cost was the plague that followed. Some believe it came with her entourage, but historians are not at all sure of that. However it came here, it stayed for almost two years, and took the lives of nearly five thousand citizens.

There had been other Royal visitors, but none had proved as costly as Elizabeth's. Some were certainly not as peaceful. Before the 1500s visiting Kings were inclined to bring an army with them, to make it plainly understood whose laws might not be broken. Civic leaders would know the King's wrath if they had failed to keep the walls and gates in good repair.

At least one royal pair of calmer disposition passed under the arch of St Stephen's Gate – Charles II and his Portuguese wife, Queen Catherine. For their visit on Thursday September 28th, 1671, the city did not overstretch its resources, but there were decorations and huge cheering crowds. Through bad weather, poor planning, and the King's own wilfulness, the visit had an unpromising start.

Opposite; a view of St Stephen's Gate from the shops close to the car park entrance, looking toward the gate, as it would appear on the traffic island. (The traffic island is below eye level.) The door high in the side of the nearest gate tower gave access to the raised walkway on the city wall. There are signs of this walkway on the ruins of the wall and mural tower to the left of this view. There is more of the city wall in the distance on Chapel Field Road.

But the people loved Catherine, and with their applause, told her so. Earlier, in 1599, one of Elizabethan England's most famous entertainers waited outside St Stephen's Gate, preparing to enter the city in a style befitting a Shakespearean actor. On the city side of the gate a huge crowd waited for Will Kemp at the end of his dance from London – his 'nine days wonder' – to dance his way into the city, and into our history. Our present day local Morris dancers, *'Kemp's Men'* are named in his memory.

St Stephen's Gate had been by far the most dramatic of all the city gates; it would have looked appropriate in the walls of a fortified Roman town. On Cuningham's prospect of the city, drawn in 1558,* the gate is shown with a long double arched bridge over the ditch, strong enough for quite heavy carts, although the arch was quite narrow. For pedestrians there were 'wickets' or 'posterns' (arched tunnels) through the bottom of both towers as footways, like those in King's Lynn's famous South Gate, but smaller.

Because of its ceremonial function, St Stephen's Gate may have been kept in better repair than some others. Before 1720, it still had high barbican walls along each edge of its bridge over the ditch, but an etching of that time shows the two round-faced towers to be in a bad state. In 1793 the gate was finally destroyed and the site swept clear. Ironically, St Stephen's was one of the first gates to be removed, and yet, had it been preserved, it would have proved no hindrance to modern traffic. It would have stood harmlessly on the northeast half of St Stephen's traffic island. Late in the twentieth century, with no consideration for the history hidden there, the road junction was ripped apart to build subway tunnels for pedestrians and the huge traffic island we have today.

* See references, page 71

St Giles' Gate

The country track outside this gate was the way to Watton and Hingham, with no direct connections to more important towns and cities, but it became important as a gate for local farmers.

The first St Giles' Church is mentioned in the Domesday Book, but little remains of the repairs made in 1165. St. Giles' Hospital, sited near the gate, was originally for cripples and beggars, who were allowed to use St Giles' Street as their route to the market. In 1308 a leprosarium was founded close to the outside of the gate, on a site opposite to the present day Catholic Cathedral.

The present church of St Giles' dates from 1420 and the Upper St Giles' area was well built-up by the 1500s. In that century the gate was known as Newport Gate. At that time, there was still a bridge over the ditch edged with barbican walls. The road over it and through the gate offered travellers and traders two routes to the market, Upper Newport (Bethel Street) and Lower Newport (St. Giles' Street). At the market both streets ended with a steep downward slope, one at each end of the market square, so traders finished their cart-hauling journeys with ease, but ascending homeward was another matter. Hopefully the carts were then lighter.

The outside of the gate from a corner of the pedestrian bridge over Grapes Hill. Had the gate survived, a special base would have been needed to support the gatehouse while Grapes Hill was being excavated for the new road. The two big buildings, one on each side of the gate, were there before the gate was demolished.

The market in those days was just as busy and crowded as it is now. It is said that the street we now call Upper St Giles' was used as an overflow, wide enough to serve as a street market and still have space for carts and wagons to pass through – very convenient for some of the stallholders selling their country produce, having come directly through this gate from outlying farms.

Newport Gate, like many other city gates, could never have looked anything but dull, even to the most enthusiastic historian, but Lower Newport Street (St Giles' Street) had became rather grand by the early 1700s, with an almost continuous line of fine houses. Some were the homes of people whose names should be better known, great public benefactors, physicians, surgeons and chemists.

Dr Edward Rigby was a specialist gallstone surgeon, who also convinced the civic authorities of the importance of vaccination. His surgery was in St Giles' Street, and he also had an apothecary shop in Pit Lane (named for the refuse pit which had earlier been part of the *Willow Lane cockey)*, but since renamed *Rigby Court*. Sir Frederick Bateman, an eye surgeon, invented an important surgical instrument; Harry Woodcock was a surgeon and dental specialist.

These are only some of the doctors and surgeons of St Giles' Street in the 1700s, the earliest professional residents in an area which the citizens of a later century would call *'The Harley Street of Norwich'*.

Among other benefactors was Mary Chapman, who founded the Bethel hospital in 1714, thereby prompting a change of street name. Her hospital was *'For the care of curable lunatics'*.

Thirty-five years later the worsted weaver Thomas Churchman designed and laid out part of Chapelfield Gardens and gave it an avenue of elm trees. They are long gone, replaced by later plantings, but his house is still there on the corner of Bethel Street, where Cleveland Road sweeps round into St Giles' Street from Chapelfield. This well preserved Georgian building, *Churchman House,* is now the registrar's office.

Side by side with ordinary citizens, these remarkable people may have passed daily under the arch of St Giles' Gate, taking care on wet days to avoid spouts of water draining from the gatehouse roof.

From the hermit room, looking through an arched window on the city side of the gate one could see over the roof tops, the 112 feet tower of St Giles' church; the tallest church tower in the city, with a fire beacon on its top, used at the time of Kett's Rebellion.

We know from a drawing by Henry Ninham that the tall three-storey buildings on each side of the gate, were there before it was demolished, as were the Queen's Head and King's Head public houses. The pubs date from 1760, but the buildings that housed them are from a much earlier time, as are many other surviving buildings in this street.

By 1789, more houses had been built against the city wall, all the way down Grapes Hill. Outside the wall, the ditch had been filled, levelled, and made into gardens. Pedestrians on their way into the city, had the arch of St Giles' Gate to walk through for just three more years. Then the character of the street changed profoundly.

With the removal of the gate, the area outside it was open and available. Outside the street a new prison was built, because Norwich Castle was no longer suitable, but the new purpose built prison served for less than sixty years. It was demolished, and in 1884 Bishop Riddell laid the foundation stone of what was to become the impressive Catholic cathedral church of St John, a second cathedral for our city. Builders worked on it for twenty-six years and it was dedicated in 1910. In its authentic Gothic style, it looks much older than its years, and visitors find it hard to believe it is such a young building. Yet its foundations were laid ninety-one years after the gate was swept away.

For the widening of Grapes Hill in the 1970s, the old road was lowered by many feet. By that action we lost information about the city ditch and the bridge that had for centuries linked this gate to the country outside the city.

The view along the street toward the city side of the gate. The gate would have been somewhat humbled by the huge St John's Roman Catholic Cathedral.

St Benedict's Gate

This city gate stood over the main road from the market towns to the west. For the Romans it was an important marching road, and was probably used by the Iceni people before them. From a Saxon settlement the road gained the name Upper Westwyck. To some locals this was 'Heaven's Gate', being a favoured gathering place for pilgrims setting out for Walsingham. Other processions set out from here; local clergy would annually lead their parishioners to a holy cross outside the city, and others carried provisions to an alms house, and the leper hospital of Saint Benedict.

The citizens of this area had a number of churches in which to celebrate their faith; St Gregory's, St Margaret's, St Swithin's, St Benedict's. The great church of St Laurence stands by the site of a staithe where herrings were landed from river barges, when the Wensum was much wider than it is now. Now three of those churches have other worthy uses; St Swithin's is an art centre, St Margaret's is used for exhibitions, and St Gregory's is a music and drama centre.

In 1549, John Dudley, Earl of Warwick, brought part of his army through this gate, in his campaign to recapture the city from Kett's rebels. The wagon drivers and gun crews must have been skilful, for the arch was narrow.

Like St Stephen's, this gate too had ceremonial importance; it was another royal way into the city. Henry VI came in 1448 and 1449; Edward IV's Queen, Elizabeth Woodville, brought her daughters here for several days in July, 1469. The gate was decorated and an elaborate stage was set with banners, crowns and modelled images of angels and giants.

The view from Barn Road. In the distance,
St John's Roman Catholic Cathedral.

Over a hundred years later, our first Queen Elizabeth passed through St Benedict's during her stay here in 1578. As the historian Blomefield tells us, the gate was grandly decorated *'with herbs and flowers, with garlands, rich cloths, and a thousand devices.'* She passed through the gate twice; once to hunt in the deer park in Costessey, and again some days later with great ceremony, to continue her Royal Progress.

It is only a short step to some historic sites remaining in this street. The Queen of Hungary was a pub occupying the house of a medieval merchant, now well cared for as a flower shop and private home. The Plough was a merchant's premises of the 1600s. These and the Three Kings pub were there before the gate was demolished.

Sadly, many old buildings were lost to make way for tram lines at the start of the twentieth century, but that was nothing compared to the damage done to this area by the bombing raids in World War II. The target was the nearby City Station, at that time an important railway terminal, but they also hit the homes and shops of Barn Road and St Benedict's Street. St Benedict's church tower, now alone on open ground, is a reminder of those terrible times.

St Benedict's Gate had a stair turret built onto the side of its south-facing wall. By a sideways extension some time after 1720, this was incorporated into the main body of the gate. After demolition in 1793, only the south side of the archway survived, complete with a hinge pin of one of its doors. (This was only because part of a house had been built over it.) When the road was widened in 1930, a new footpath was made possible by cutting an archway through the ancient wall, but it was all blown away in the same bombing raid that destroyed the walls of St Benedict's Church.

Heigham Gate

This little gate was set into the lowest lying part of the city wall. The city guide and historian R. H. Mottram, had this to say about the river bank and the gate;

*'..a dismal appearance... swampy and unapproachable...
...a mean building, never a passage for much traffic...'*

Long before the city gates and walls were built, there had been Appleyard's water-powered corn mills on the river bank, and new mills had been built nearby by 1430. Millers carrying corn or flour through this gate could only use small carts, so they probably made little use of it. It was more practical for the millers to use the river Wensum for transport. In medieval times the river was wide and braided, but it was clearly ideal for the barges carrying fish for the market, clay for the kilns in Pottergate, and leather and other materials for the tanners and dyers. In time the dyers *('letesteres'* or *'litesters')* dominated the city side of the river and called it *Letesteres Row.* From the dyers' operations began Norwich's cloth industries.

From Saxon times, land adjacent to Heigham Gate belonged to St Benet's Abbey. From the late 1300s there were disputes between the Abbot and the city council, and that may have something to do with locals calling it 'Hell Gate.'

A reconstruction of the gate looking into the city. It is based on Kirkpatrick's 1720 etching, but showing the gate as it may originally have been built, with battlements and an angled barbican protecting access from the gatehouse to the walkway.

One of those disputes indirectly brought about the brief imprisonment of Norwich's worthy mayor and merchant, Robert Toppes, of King Street.

The local character of the Wensum changed continuously through the centuries. The Saxons had named an island further down stream (opposite Robert Gybson Way) *Coslany,* meaning *Cost's Long Island* or *Cost's Land.* The Cleer-Kirkpatrick map of 1696 shows the same single island close to Coslany Bridge, while T. Smith's map in Chase's 1783 directory shows two more islands linked by a river crossing. It is possible that the piers of a stone bridge built in 1521 caused some silting, thereby creating additional islands.

A 1720 view of the gatehouse* by John Kirkpatrick is finely etched, but with no indication of which side he had drawn. A view including the city ditch would have told us, but most of it had been filled-in by then. There are clues.

Piercing the battlements to the left of the gatehouse are arrow-slits *(loops)*, but no walkway *(alure)*. Presumably the walkway was on the other side of the wall. Another clue is in the absence of buildings beyond the archway, although there are houses in front of it. The John Crosshold map of 1707, dated only thirteen years earlier, shows open land on the city side of the gate, and rows of houses close to the gate on the other side; further indicating that Kirkpatrick looked toward the city, and the outside face of the gate.

Sometime before he made his etching, the gatehouse battlements were removed and replaced with a tiled roof, and an arcade was cut through the wall as an additional access. 22 years after Kirkpatrick's etching, the gate arch was enlarged to ten feet wide and thirteen feet high to its apex, indicating a need to let wider and taller loads through the gate. The gate was demolished between 1792 and 1800.

* See 'Views of the gates of Norwich' (Fitch)
  as listed in 'References', page 71

Coslany Gate

This gate, dating from about 1275, was the most westerly in the city's north wall. It was built close to a difficult low-lying riverside area and led to the route to the villages of Drayton and Taverham. The arch was less than 12 feet high, smaller than some others. Known as Coslany Gate, (pronounced *Cosny*), it stood at the junction now known as St Martin at Oak.

The bridge over the ditch was one of those with barbican walls at its sides. The city wall here may not have had a wallwalk, although in 1522, the gate was re-armed against a possible invasion by the French.

This small gate must have proved a problem to the Earl of Warwick early in the morning of August 27th, 1549. He had to get his army out of the city to face Kett's rebels waiting outside the north wall; the other north wall gates were too close to the enemy lines. No matter what, his men had to struggle through this constricting arch.

Cosny Gate saw some colourful events. Here within the city wall, along the narrow St Martin at Oak Wall Lane was a big open area called *'Justin's Acre'*.

A view from the south-west corner of Baker's Road, looking toward the city. In the upper right corner of the gate is a small window which gave some light to the steps going up from the hermit room to the roof. Beside the right hand buttress of the gatehouse is the Dun Cow public house, standing where its predecessor stood more than two hundred years ago, when the gate was still there. Beside the gate and the old pub is a lane leading to the river; down there, at the rear of the pub, is the stub of a mural tower.

In the 1300s this was a field for tournaments, a place where men-at-arms would show off their battle skills.

Most dramatically, lance-bearing armoured knights on fast horses, jousted in contests, for this was, correctly named, the 'Jousting Field.' Throughout England, tournament days attracted huge crowds of city and country folk. There were warm-up events like bear-baiting and cock-fights, and throughout the day there would be archery contests, sword duels, wrestling and the extra sport of throwing unpleasant things at minor criminals locked in the stocks. There may well have been a ducking stool for calming 'scolding' wives.

In other words, fun days, medieval style.

Some citizens entered into hazardous contests with swordsmen and wrestlers; they could also test themselves against a *'quintain'*, a device used by knights to keep themselves tournament-skilled. This was a two-yard long bar, pivoted on a tall stout pole, at the shoulder height of a mounted rider. At one end of the bar was a target board, at the other end, a bag of sand. The rider charged; if he was fast and hit the target squarely with his lance, the bag of sand would swing harmlessly behind him; otherwise it would knock him off his horse.

There was an added attraction on St Valentine's day here in 1340. King Edward III came with his wife Queen Philippa to watch their son Edward the Prince of Wales (the Black Prince) in tournament – extra training perhaps for the war in France.

The Coslany Gate absorbed the echoes of weapons clashing in battle, crowds cheering and, for hundreds of years after that, the murmur and rustle of everyday life. It survived until 1808, one of the last to be taken down.

St Augustine's Gate

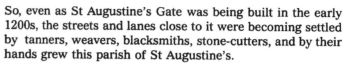

From the 2nd century BC., the area north of the River Wensum was open country. A Roman family set up a farmstead and left a copper lamp, a coin and some pottery to tell us they were here. The countryside remained wide open, and was farmed throughout Saxon times. A farmstead called *The Lathes*, founded by a monastery, is recalled now in a housing estate bearing its name. In what became Botolph Street (now under Anglia Square) there was a wood called *'Mereholt'* and beside it the *'Pynfolde'* where stray cattle and horses were held. Beyond the northern city wall, tracks that we would hardly call roads wound their way among fields and streams to the villages of Hellesdon and Horsford, to Aylsham, Holt and the coast, where there were markets to be supplied with goods made in the city.

The city side of the gate. The square window above the arch was bigger than in some gates. The two tall windows to the left of the arch gave light to steps up to the hermit room. The street door to these steps must have been in the buttress at the left hand corner of the tower. Just visible on the right, behind the gate, is the turning into Magpie and Waterloo roads. The Catherine Wheel public house is on the extreme right hand edge of the sketch. Visible through the opening beside the pub is a section of city wall. The other side of that can be seen from Magpie Road, where it was exposed when the premises of the Magpie Printers were removed.

So, even as St Augustine's Gate was being built in the early 1200s, the streets and lanes close to it were becoming settled by tanners, weavers, blacksmiths, stone-cutters, and by their hands grew this parish of St Augustine's.

The parish became self-sufficient, with a measure of independence from the rest of the city south of the River. Not far from the gate was a place for citizens to pay their 'geld' or taxes, the *Gildencroft*; there too was a sports and recreation area, and the 'Tabor's Folly' where musicians played *'...for youths and their maidens...'* on *'tabors'* (drums) and *'tuckets'* (trumpets).

Some needy citizens were cared for in a two storey house built onto a rectangular mural tower in Baker's Road, only a little way from the gate, a home for the care and treatment of lepers. A part of the tower is still there, among the ruins of the city wall. It was the hospital of St Mary and St Clement, founded it is said by Margaret, Countess of Lincoln. Norwich, like most cities, had many such *leprosaria.*

While St Augustine's Gate was still standing, some notable people lived in the parish. By his will of 1617, Thomas Anguish set up schools for the city's poorest children, and John Gurney, by an act of parliament in 1720, managed to get a ban on the import of calico garments from India, thus saving work for local weavers. Two brothers of the same Gurney family opened their first bank in *Tooley Street* (Now Pitt Street), thereby sowing the seeds of Barclays' banking empire. As time passed, shawl and shoemakers added to the skills of the parish, and their products were sold in the city, throughout England and overseas.

The gate was demolished in 1794.

Magdalen Gate

Opposite: looking into Magdalen Street from beside the Artichoke.

Magdalen Street is believed to have been part of a major Roman road, one of two that formed a crossroads in Tombland. Roman pottery was found in this street in 1974 and 1987. Anglo-Saxon coins dating back to about 900 AD, bear the place name *Norvic,* and may have been minted locally. From about 1300 it was the work place of blacksmiths, masons and iron smelters.

The gate, known then as Fyebrigge Gate, 'the way to Fye Bridge' (near Tombland) was fully built by 1339; with Barre Gate, the last to be completed. Some resident masons may have helped to build it. The street is about as wide now as it was in medieval times, and we know from old engravings that the gate was offset to the west. Like most city gates, it had small arch-topped windows facing into the city. There was a door high up in the west wall of the gate, leading out of the hermit's room onto the raised walkway of the city wall. The walkway can still be seen at the top of the wall-ruins. There may have been mural towers quite close to the sides of this gate, with only short sections of city wall leading to them, the tower to the west in Magpie Road being only 70 feet away from the gate; the tower to the east even closer at only 36 feet. An adverse turn of the wall in such places left defensive blind spots, so such towers were essential, having arrow-loops positioned for a clear line of sight along the outer face of the wall.

The Sanctuary Map of 1541 (held by Norwich Castle Museum) shows this gate with stone walls (*barbicans*) flanking the bridge, which must therefore have been supported by a stone arch. This and the towers set close to the gate show the strategic importance of this thoroughfare.

Bull Close Road, following the line of the old city ditch, has a misleading name; the 'Bull Close' was within the city on the other side of the city wall. Cattle from the close were driven through the gate and over the bridge to graze the slopes of Magdalen hill. No doubt the ditch was fenced-off; it was deep and wide. This part of it was open until about 1789.

When the Black Death first struck the city in 1349, some victims were hastily buried, fully clothed, in the graveyard of St Margaret's church. Their remains were found during an excavation in 1987. Also found buried there, face down in pits with their wrists bound, were criminals. They had been taken through the archway of Magdalen Gate to the gallows outside and brought back to the churchyard for burial.

Gallows, possibly in the same place, were used there again in 1549 for the hanging, drawing and quartering of thirty men captured at the end of Kett's Rebellion. Earl Warwick may have thought it appropriate that they should be executed there, close to the site of his decisive last battle against Kett.*

The view toward Magdalen Road. Through later subsidence, the tower needed additional support, hence the peculiar arrangement of buttresses. The Artichoke public house, in the distance on the right of the gate, stands on the site of the medieval 'Rush Fair' where poultry, piglets, and rushes were bought; the rushes were used to cover floors where we would nowadays lay carpets.

* For the author's views about the battle site, please refer to his articles in the Eastern Daily Press, July 11 and 18, 2009.

Guards on Magdalen Gate witnessed a lot of rebel action in 1549. Near there, on July 31st, the rebels captured one of the Marquis of Northampton's mercenaries and hanged him at their camp on Mousehold Heath. On Sunday August 25th, rebels broke through the wall at Bull Close and surged toward the city in an attack that alarmed Earl Warwick. A church named All Saints, at the corner of Magdalen Street and what is now Cowgate (then possibly Allderhalen street) may have been damaged during the rebellion; it was completely demolished one year later. There had been attached to it, a burial ground for the lepers of the Saint Mary Magdalen and Saint Leonard's hospitals half a mile to the north of the Magdalen Gate. At the gallows in 1615, a brutal death befell a Roman Catholic priest named Thomas Tunstall, again, hanged drawn and quartered. Following his final request, his head was carried to St Benedict's Gate, by reason of his special regard for this particular Saint. There, following the usual custom, the head was mounted on a pole on top of the gatehouse.

Brewing later became a major industry in Magdalen Street. The gate was still standing when several breweries opened here in the late 1700s. Some of them were there for a long time, and gave their names to public houses such as Hope Brewery and The Golden Dog. There were other brewers: Phoenix, Heighams, Stannards, and Pattesons.

It was on the site of St Margaret's Church, destroyed in the 1400s, that Thomas Tawell founded the first school for the blind in 1805, just three years before the Magdalen Gate was demolished. No doubt there were times when his first blind pupils had to be guided through its archway. By the time the gate was removed in 1808, its merlons and embrasures had crumbled away.

Barre Gate

In medieval times, the road from the little church of St James (now a puppet theatre) was a narrow way leading to the hamlet of Pockthorpe, and onward to Ranworth, Plumstead and South Walsham.

Work on the Barre Gate (later known as Pockthorpe gate) should have begun about 1300, but owing to a boundary dispute with the Prior of Norwich it was delayed for many years. The Benedictine Priory owned huge areas of land on the high heath, which they claimed reached as far as Magdalen Road. On the famous Cuningham prospect of 1559, that area is labelled 'Monks Wold' (since corrupted to 'Mousehold').

Most of the city gates had been built by 1288, but Barre Gate and its neighbour Magdalen Gate were not finished before 1339, and it was not until 1346, that the city was granted the last piece of land for the final 300-foot stretch of city wall, from Barre Gate to the river. However, through their late arrival the two gates may have benefited from the problems experienced at some other gates. Between 1220 and 1288 gates had been of smaller build; Magdalen and Barre Gates were built with bigger openings through their archways.

A view of the outside of the gate. There is some doubt about the true position of this gate; it is shown here on its most likely alignment, that being on the south side of the road, where the surviving houses are fairly old and may follow earlier building lines. To the right is the junction with Silver Road. The polygonal Pockthorpe Tower and part of the wall are visible from this viewpoint. The tower still has its access, and the top of the wall has fragments of walkway.

By then the defence-conscious Richard Spynk had armed the 'fighting tops' of all the other gates and towers with his 'espringall' catapults (see page 27) but owing to the delays, the unfortunate Barre Gate was overlooked and had neither shot nor weapons.

Water flowing off the 'Monks Wold' and along the city ditch to the River Wensum, proved useful to leather workers who needed running water for some of their processes. From the 1300s, tanners had built their houses and workshops here and named the two connected streets Bargate and Pockthorpe. Their skills commanded respect and by the 1500s these streets had become an area of wealth.

At the polygonal tower, the city ditch turned south and flowed by the Barre Gate, and 300 feet to the south it joined the Wensum as a minor tributary, where merchants moored their trading barges in the shelter of the last stretch of city wall, guarded by the final mural tower. Part of the wall remains, but little of the tower.

The gate was damaged by rebels in 1549, but most of its original medieval structure was unharmed and it was all promptly *'made anew.'* During the Civil War, protective measures were taken, but nothing harmful was done to the gate. In 1757, more repairs were made to the gate and the adjacent walls, and as late as 1790 a chimney was added to the north side of the gate to vent a fireplace.

Customers of the Windsor Castle, the Bird in Hand, and the Wrestlers must have walked, perhaps unsteadily, through the arch of Barre Gate; these pubs were still there when the gate was demolished in 1792. There was a slum clearance in the 1930s, and the pubs too were cleared away.

52

Bishop's Gate

Opposite; a view from the city side of the gate. The Red Lion public house is to the left.

It may be fair to say that many Norwich gates looked ugly and forbidding. Only the Bishop's Gate had the grand castle-like style of King's Lynn's famous South Gate. It was a late arrival, and architectural styles had changed. With the strong lines of its angular turrets it crowned the river crossing used by Bishops, Priors and priests; it was the exit used by pilgrims to St Michael's and St William's chapels, and the Priory of St Leonard's; it welcomed dignitaries to the Bishop's Palace and the Benedictine Priory, and those on merciful missions to Bishop Suffield's Great Hospital of St Giles'. For all that, it was the first to be demolished.

Long before a stone bridge was built here, the Romans may have had a wooden bridge over the Wensum to join the road on the other side of the river with their gravel-hardened causeway over the riverside meadows and their crossroads in what later became Tombland. Some of the causeway is still under Bishopgate Street.

In a detailed document of 1342,* acknowledging the importance of all the defensive work given to the city by Richard Spynk, we are told that part of the river crossing was a drawbridge, and that bars and chains were provided for the gate. The drawbridge may have been as shown here, or within the main body of the tower.

* In 'Records of the City of Norwich'.
See references, page 77

The battlements at the roof of the gate seem to have been set rather low to be effective. Of the four turrets, only those at the city face of the gate had stairways built into them.

The skilled craftsmen, stone masons and carpenters, occupied in building the Cathedral and Priory, stone by stone, in the late 11th and early 12th centuries, and their successors, worked constantly on alterations and additions to the main buildings. They settled and made their homes near the Barre Gate and along the length of Holme Street (now Bishopgate).

Just outside the Bishop's Gate was the Lollards' Pit, an old chalk quarry abandoned for 300 years, until the civic authorities found a terrible use for it – burnings at the stake, a punishment for heretics required by law. Its first victim was William White, who, being a follower of John Wycliffe, preached against the established beliefs of the church and was burned there with two others in 1428. They were known as Lollards, hence the name of the pit. Then there were early protestants such as Thomas Bilney, and at least sixty victims of the Catholic Queen Mary's five year reign of persecution. As part of the 'legal process' lists were kept of those sent to the flames. In all of England during those years, only London and Canterbury saw more such executions.

Lollards' pit was so used for 150 years. That fearful progress from the Guildhall prison, through the city to Holme Street, under the arch of the Bishop's Gate and over the bridge to the Lollards' Pit, was witnessed by a multitude of Norwich citizens, sometimes with cruel glee and sometimes in solemn silence.

In 1549 the gate was bombarded by Kett's rebels. It was soon rebuilt, although it was never as strong as it had been, and neither was the bridge. Two hundred years later the bridge foundations and two of the bridge arches, including the one directly under the gate, were found to be urgently in need of repair. Worse still, the entire gate was leaning to the north. By then people were also complaining about the gate arch; like the other gates, it was too small for bigger carts and wagons to pass through.

So, finally, in 1792, the decision was made to take it down. No doubt the residents of the riverside houses beside the gate were pleased to see it go; it would no longer shade their houses or dominate their street. Eased of the weight of the gate, the bridge was the more easily repaired, but early in the 1900s we almost lost that too. Planners and councillors wanted to destroy it and replace it with something wider for bigger and heavier traffic. In 1923, antiquarians and other caring people successfully campaigned for its protection. They saved the bridge and some other ancient buildings. From their work evolved the highly valued Norwich Society.

The view from the riverside moorings.

The Water Gate

Bishop Herbert de Losinga, the first Bishop of Norwich, being a Norman, knew the fine quality of stone quarried in that part of Normandy called Caen, and wanted it for his new cathedral in Norwich; and so, in 1096, it was ordered. It was cut to size in Caen and sent to Yarmouth where it was loaded onto river barges, up to 30 tons per barge, and brought up to Norwich. It could not be carted over the water-softened meadow, so a canal was dug from the river to the Lower Close. A staithe was built there where, using simple cranes, the stone was off-loaded. To prevent unlawful use of the waterway, massive doors were kept closed at the head of the staithe.

In December and January, in the relative warmth of their workshops, the masons marked out and carved the stones into their final shapes. Building work was done in the period from February to November. On September 29th, 1101, the presbytery, transepts and part of the nave were complete enough for dedication. In 1119 the bishop died, but a succession of Bishops continued the work of completing the cathedral, adding to it, carrying out alterations and repairs right up to the present day.

The first water-gate may have been built very early, soon after the cutting of the canal. Being Norman, it would have been quite symmetrical, with a round tower at each end of the arch.

Opposite; a view from the Ferry Staithe, looking toward the city. The canal is fully in view through the arch. Norwich Cathedral is in the distance to the right of the water-gate.

A house was built onto one end of the water-gate in the late 1500s. It would have been then that a tower was removed and an extra arch added for pedestrian use.

A cathedral chorister named John Sandling was one of the first ferrymen, and served from 1582 to 1597. Part of his duty may have been to the Bishop and other church dignitaries, not for simple river crossings – they had the Bishop's Bridge for that – but for longer river journeys far into the county.

Sandling lived to the age of 89; then there followed a succession of ferrymen, but it was known for long thereafter as Sandling's Ferry. The attached house was used as an Inn. By then the canal was no longer navigable; it had become blocked with weeds and mud. To render it serviceable again would have been too expensive, so in 1780 it was filled and its course levelled, thereby making a convenient road for ferry users. Ten years later a man named John Pull became the ferryman. He ran the service and the inn from 1790 until 1841; he died in 1842, having been the longest serving of all the ferrymen. At his death, the licence for the inn was not renewed. Interestingly there had been published in 1834, eight years before his death, a plan for building the Thorpe Railway Station on the ferry side of the river. Had that plan been adopted, this famous landmark and popular piece of Norwich history would have been swept away. Again, Norwich was fortunate and Pull's Ferry was able to serve the citizens until 1943, just two years before the end of World War II. Walking from the Lower Close into the Ferry Road, some evidence of the watercourse can be seen. The oldest houses in the row, numbers 27, 30 and 31, were built well back from the edge of the canal; later structures are closer or over the edge of it.

58

The Boom Towers

From Carrow Bridge the ruins of these towers can be seen on opposite banks of the River Wensum. Originally there may have been only the west tower as an appropriate end to the length of wall leading down to the river from King Street Gate. The second or east tower was not built until 1344, as part of Richard Spynk's contribution to the city defences. It had an interesting arrangement of three turrets, not characteristic of other city towers.

A steep, narrow footpath leads down between young trees and shrubs to the river bank, and from there it is a short walk to the more prominent east tower. From the river bank it can be seen that the towers are not directly opposite each other, which seems peculiar. It may be due to a setting-out error, or perhaps it was intended that both towers should align with the city wall, which does not lie at a right-angle to the river.

As part of the city defences, Richard Spynk provided stout chains to be laid across the river between the towers, and a windlass in the west tower by which to tension them; this would be an effective control of approaching river craft, later used to enable the collection of toll charges. There were many similar harbour towers elsewhere in Britain, where it was necessary to control the movement of shipping. Indeed, they declare the importance of such harbours. Blockhouses held a chain over the River Fowey in Cornwall; for Portsmouth there was a chain-bearing round tower and a blockhouse, and similar blockhouses for Dartmouth and Plymouth harbours.

Opposite; the view from the east bank of the river. To the left is King Street Gate and in the distance, the so called 'Black Tower' of Bracondale.

In all of these, the heavy chains were simply drawn taut over harbour mouths, a considerable strain on towers and winches. For our relatively narrow River Wensum, it was possible to lift the chain by the method shown opposite or something similar. Naval equipment such as the heavy timbers, blocks and tackle, were relatively easy to acquire and install. Chains of 'good Spanish steel' were prescribed, and must have been heavy, although the winding gear itself, be it capstan or windlass, would have been quite simple. In such installations anywhere, the lowered chains rested on river bed or harbour mud, and were subject to fouling; no doubt the chains gradually deteriorated.

In *The Walls of Norwich,* a 1910 report to the city council, it is suggested that the Boom Towers were so named because *'a boom at some time did the same duty as the chain'.* However, such an installation would be heavy, complicated and expensive. It seems unlikely. There is another quite obvious explanation for the use of the name. Some of these towers elsewhere had naval guns for giving warning shots to possibly hostile approaching vessels; imagine the 'boom' of a powerful gun discharging in such a confined space; words migrate, and mutate into new and inappropriate uses.

By 1938 one of the turrets on the east tower had fallen, leaving two that looked like horns. Seen against the evening sky, its silhouette had all the style of a huge satanic figure; no wonder the ruin became known as the 'Devil's tower.' There are early photographs of ships off-loading their freight at nearby staithes; in one of these, the tower has only one remaining turret. By 1955 there were no turrets at all, and since then, the deterioration has continued. Curiously, in the base of this tower in the 1800s, there remained what appeared to be a staple to secure a chain.

During the last years of the gates, the west tower became a cinder oven for making fuel blocks from coal dust, much of that raw material being readily to hand at many coal depots.

The Castle Gates

It was important to the Norman conquerors that the Saxon English should quickly learn who were their new masters and accept Norman rule. Castles were built throughout the realm, first with timber on earth mounds, with wooden curtain walls surrounding the summits, and ditches all round the mounds.

Norwich Castle was begun in 1067, a year after the Battle of Hastings. The Norman overlords made do with a wooden castle for less than fifty years, by which time their grand and imposing stone keep was more or less finished; certainly well enough in 1122 for Henry I to spend Christmas there. By about 1270 the wooden palisades had been replaced by stone walls, stone watch-towers, a stone bridge over the ditch, and stone gates. And yet, a century later, the castle had become the county gaol, and the massive stoneworks had more to do with the holding of prisoners than any military purpose.

Of the gates in this view, the nearest stood on the crest of a semi circular bank. Castle Hill, the pedestrian approach to the bridge, is over part of it. It was between the castle ditch and another ditch now occupied by the Castle Mall shopping centre. The gate had a drawbridge it could lay over it; you can see the chain ports above its archway. Part of the gate was unearthed during the castle mall excavations of 1987 to 1991.

Seen here are the entrance gates to the castle keep, viewed from the highest point of the Castle Mall Gardens. There were perhaps as many as ten more gates in the walls enclosing a wide area round the castle mound, and as many towers. The blockhouses now at the lower end of the castle bridge are not shown in this view; they date from a much later time.

The gate at the higher or castle end of the stone bridge had round 'drum' towers each side of its archway, the bases of which are still there beside the upper corners of the bridge. This gate too, had a drawbridge, perhaps twenty feet long. Each of these gates had a portcullis. Beyond the drum towers on the right hand side of the keep is the enclosed stone stairway to its first floor entrance.

In time, the mile-wide city, once so dependent upon the Castle for its protection, built its own defences – the walls, towers and gates described in this book.

A succession of monarchs re-fortified the castle, and yet by 1609 it was declared to be badly decayed. During the Civil War the Parliamentarians strengthened the keep, but removed the stone walls surrounding the castle mound to provide clear lines of sight for their ordnance. After that there was a long period of decay. The battlements of the roofless keep crumbled, and sections of the Caen stone facing fell away. In the 1820s a new gaol was built beside the keep to ease overcrowding. The original castle bridge was replaced.

As part of a five year repair programme that began in 1834, the keep was refaced with Bath stone. Some academics were not pleased with the result; the new stonework had been extended downward over the lower sections of the wall, which had originally been exposed flint. The number of battlements had also been changed; there had been thirteen on each wall of the keep; after renovations there were only nine, and it is those that we see at the present day.

The problem of the overcrowded prison ended with the building of a new prison outside St Giles' Street in 1887, at which time the city bought the keep and gaol to redevelop as our museum and art gallery. For several hundred years the citizens had been busy putting to their own use more and more of the old castle lands; the meadow had become the livestock market, serving that purpose until 1960.

Cow Tower

Below; the tower before it was damaged by Kett's Rebels in 1549. In the distance, Hassett's Hall, reconstructed for this view.

The monks of the Benedictine Priory were the first to build on this meadow site, using a simple tower for the collection of tolls from river traffic in support of the Great Hospital. Like the Boom Towers at Carrow, it may have had chains that could be raised over the river. Later it was the priory prison; *The Dungeon Tower.*

The tower was granted to the city in 1378, and in the 1380s was refaced by Robert Snape, who used bricks inside and out, to cover the flint core of the original toll house. It was completed by 1390. The city needed the tower as part of its riverside defences; it is one of the earliest surviving examples in England of a freestanding brick-faced medieval military tower. From within its massive walls, crossbows and handguns could be aimed through its many gun ports and archery loops, and from its fighting top, men using *espringalls* and *arblasters*, could launch heavy round shot.

The tower was strategically placed at the bend in the river, and from its height of almost 50 feet, men on its fighting top had a clear view up the steep slopes of Mousehold and for some distance southward down river, and westward up river toward the Barre or Pockthorpe Gate. It was on open ground well away from other defensive buildings; the nearest was the Bishop's Gate on Bishop's Bridge, so for the comfort of the soldiers stationed within, the tower had fireplaces, privies and a communal dining area. Sleeping quarters were on upper floors, convenient for urgent action at the fighting top and the higher gun-ports. The fighting top was destroyed by Kett's cannons in the 1549 rebellion.

Following the Dissolution of the monasteries, William Blenner-Hassett from Horsford, leased some priory land north of the river opposite the tower, and in about 1547 built Hassett's Hall. The tower was included in the lease, and became *Hassett's Tower.* The hall was demolished in 1792.

On almost all maps from the 1500s the tower is named after the surrounding meadow, which was long known as Cow Holme (the place for cows). Cow Tower now belongs to the City of Norwich, and is managed by English Heritage.

In the Final Years

In 1808, a score of men took carts, ladders, hammers and crowbars to the Magdalen Gate to do what they had already done to all the other city gates. The wrecking crews had begun in 1791, by demolishing the Bishop's Gate. It must have been dangerous work; its position on the narrow bridge made access difficult, and with its four turrets it was one of the highest gates. The men constantly faced the risk of falling into the Wensum from the parapets or scaffolding. Some months later, in 1792, wreckers began their work on the nearby Barre Gate. In that same year another crew destroyed the St Giles and Brazen Gates, and in 1793, St Stephen's and St Benedict's. A year later, it was the turn of King Street and St Augustine's Gates, and some time about then the little gate at Heigham Street – and so the destruction went on. Demolishing the gates was so much cheaper than repairing them, but fourteen more years would pass before the Ber Street, Coslany and Magdalen Gates were to be destroyed. Perhaps adequate funding had to be found for even that final task.

Early in the morning at Magdalen Gate, one may imagine that the wreckers drew their carts across the thoroughfare to block the way. They then warned the residents, shopkeepers, innkeepers and the blind pupils at Thomas Tawell's school, that dust would cloud the air for a few days.

They first removed the heavy oak doors, and set them aside; if good, they could be used elsewhere. The portcullis and its long unused windlass had been discarded years earlier. Using the gate entrance and stairways, they reached what remained of its badly crumbled fighting-top. They were reminded to save any reusable material, such as the stone or tile capping from the merlons and embrasures, and the slabs of ashlar that had formed the sides of the merlons.

At this gate most of those had already crumbled, so with cries of 'Beware below!' they set to work with their long-handled heavy hammers, to remove what remained of the parapets. The rubble fell noisily to the ground. They cut and rolled up any roofing lead that remained, lashed rope around the heavy rolls of it, and lowered them over the sides of the gate. Almost certainly the boards over the roofing timbers had decayed too, and were easy to remove. The most dangerous task was the removal of the roof beams. They were all heavy, but the spine-like centre beam, spanning the space between the city side and outer side of the gate, was the heaviest and at least eighteen feet long. Joists up to ten feet long and sloping down to the east and west of the centre beam, possibly twelve to each side, had been jointed into the sides of it.*

On ladders, the men dislodged the joints and used ropes to lower the beams to the hermit room floor, where they were temporarily stacked. Then they used their hammers again to batter the gatehouse walls down to hermit floor level. Although repaired some fifty years earlier, decades of rain, frost and settlement had probably weakened the mortar, making the task easier.

The hermit room floor in Magdalen Gate was probably wood, not masonry, although the arrangement of the timbers would have been simpler than those in the roof structure, with the joists resting directly onto the side walls of the archway. Of all the gates, Magdalen appears to have had the widest but shallowest curve of arch, so its opening may not have had vaulted masonry over it.

After the timbers of the hermit room floor were removed, what remained of Magdalen Gate was then open to the sky. All that the army of workmen had to do then was batter down the last of the walls. Armed with their big hammers, it was a simple but arduous task.

After the gates were taken down and the huge heaps of rubble were sorted and carted away, those parts of the city

* See illustrations, page 18.

wall not already officially demolished, also became quarries for useful building stone. The material was easy to remove. As with the gates, centuries of rain and frost had loosened the mortar and many a house, garden wall and even some public buildings benefited from their decay. It is only by the stubborn strength and great mass of the lower portions that so much wall has survived. 'Robbing-out' as historians call it, is no longer likely, but the exposed mortar of the walls is still subject to the ravages of time. Plants such as buddleia and sycamore make lime mortar a bed for their roots, which grow quietly and destructively, and winter frosts cause falls of flint. It has cost time and money to keep the walls in good order.

The presence of the sections of ruined wall defines the medieval shape of the city and all will be well as long as they survive. They should, for they are now protected as ancient monuments; indeed the Ancient Monuments Society considers them as important as the walls of York and Chester. Much preservation work has been done after some prompting by the Norfolk and Norwich Archaeological Society, and the Norwich Society, who in 1969 presented an exhibition entitled *'Norwich – A Walled City.'* Since then much more of the wall along Chapelfield has been revealed and preserved. In 2010 and early 2011, Carrow's eastern Boom Tower was given some belated conservation work, but it is only in Ber Street, where traffic flows into Bracondale, that we have a section of the wall still standing to its full height.

The carefully dressed and coursed stone ashlars of York's monumental gates and walls are strong and resistent to weathering, but our broken walls of flint cobbles are less durable. The strength of such walls is due mainly to the great mass of the masonry. That is the principle the Romans adopted when using the flint that came so readily to hand for their walled town at Caistor St Edmund's, and their forts of the 'Saxon Shore' such as Burgh Castle.

In further comparison with the walls of York, we see a big difference in the alures. On York's walls they are in most places luxuriously wide; on our walls all were hideously narrow. How much more massive, also, are York's battlements; their merlons and embrasures gave much better cover for their soldiers. All this has prompted the suggestion that our walls were built more for effect than serious defence. Certainly they looked strong from the outside, but people within the city would have noted the weaknesses, and soldiers on the alures, even with the width increased with timber, would have found actions with their weapons rather difficult. Spynk no doubt felt he must draw the line somewhere, and kept the project as simple as possible. He provided many mural towers, and yet in places the walls are simple to the extent that they were built with only a single leaf, and therefore with no arcade upon which to build alures. This seems to have been the case between King Street Gate and the western Boom Tower at Carrow, and for the eastward stretch of wall from Magdalen Gate to its nearest mural tower.

The last length of city wall to be legally demolished was at Heigham Gate, as late as 1853. In 1910 a piece of the wall (or a fragment of the gate) was found under the floor of number 76 Barn Road, a shop on the corner of Westwick Street. Presumably the fragment was still there until that devastating bombing raid of 1942.

While Norwich made dramatic changes to its urban landscape, the latter half of the 1700s was also a particularly changeful time throughout the world. There was a growing awareness of the trading prospects in an emerging global economy. Important discoveries were made in science and technology, and provided practical inventions for industry. Explorations, such as Cook's Pacific voyages of 1768 and 1772 and Norfolk-born Vancouver's exploits in the Pacific north-west of Canada in 1793 had far-reaching consequences.

The American colonies were lost, but Britain acquired new lands in India and Canada. Medical knowledge advanced and the population of the world grew from 750 million in 1750 to 880 million in 1800. For all the changes the gates had seen throughout more than 600 years, there had been very little to affect the growing population of Norwich – except bubonic plague and other epidemics.

Plagues periodically affected the levels of city population for at least three hundred years. Successive generations of citizens lived with the fearful prospect of their own horrifying deaths. During times of plague, the city gates were closed and barred. It is hard to imagine the terrible sense of confinement in a plague-ridden city of filthy narrow streets, but the solid dark oak doors tucked under the gate arches may have limited the spread of the disease, by holding infected people in the city. At the onset of each occurrence of plague, the wealthy were able to retire hurriedly to the less populated countryside, before the gates were ordered to be closed. There may have been very few years in which the country overall was totally free of plague, but there were no more epidemics in Britain after the terrible 'visitation' of 1665, the London scene of which was so vividly described by Daniel Defoe in his *Journal of the Plague Year.* Nonetheless, the population of Norwich had steadily climbed, reaching thirty three thousand by 1750, then slowing a little to reach 40,000 by 1800.

In the late 1700s, in the final years of the gates, there were significant changes to many streets, through buildings being converted to commercial use. This had long been a prosperous city with areas of elegant housing and formal gardens, but there began a movement out of the city by those wealthy enough to commission grand houses in such areas as Newmarket and Ipswich Roads. One city street, St Giles' was still well regarded for its fine houses and its road wide enough for their carriages (though the gate archway was barely so). Other streets were narrow and deeply medieval in character.

King Street with its river staithes was bound to hold on to its association with water-borne trading. R. H. Mottram wrote that it was *'The street most connected with the sea'.* The names of some of its most famous (or infamous) pubs reflected this; *The Ship, The Steam Packet, The Keel and Wherry,* and the *Old Barge Inn.* The street had many more pubs than those 'sailors' moorings'.' More than twenty were stretched along the length of it. Such pubs were a natural progression from the alehouses of medieval England and became a feature of many other parts of the city; Ber Street, St Stephen's, Magdalen Street and Barrack Street. They were all within easy walking distance of the of the city gates.

Chase's Norwich Directory of 1783 has in its lists for Ber Street about fifteen premises involved in the meat trade; most were butchers' shops. It may already have been known as 'Blood and Guts Street.' It was so known a hundred years later, but also by then for its uncontrolled violence.

The worsted industry, combing, spinning, weaving and dyeing, was the mainstay of Norwich wealth in 1750; it had been a source of work for East Anglians since medieval times. By 1771 there was at least one hand-loom in very many of the long-windowed top floors of the twelve thousand homes in the city, providing low-paid work for thousands of weavers, and goods to be sold in as many as fifty outlets and tailors' workshops in the streets leading to the gates. The weavers' pay was so low that whole families had to work long hours to earn enough to survive. But even that meagre life-style was to be under threat before the end of the century. Two simple words signified coming change: coal and cotton.

The slave-powered cotton plantations of the New World colonies were able to sell their crops cheaply to the coal and water-powered mills of Lancashire. From those simple, white, fluffy balls the new factories were able to produce a cloth much cheaper than was possible from wool.

There was little point in our local merchants competing

for the imported cotton, for the county had neither the readily available coal nor the topography for fast-flowing mill streams. Cotton cloth soon outsold wool cloth. The subsequent reduction of the worsted industry brought the city and county into a general decline. As our ancient gates were dying, so too was much of the local industrial base.

As builders removed cart loads of flint from demolished city walls and gates, a diverse range of goods from around the world was arriving at staithes and warehouses in King Street. Wherries and keels, destined to rule the waterways for another century, carried trade goods between Yarmouth and Norwich; Norfolk was slowly emerging from the 1780s decline of its worsted industry.

The removal of our city gates produced a very great change to the appearance of Norwich, and in that we may see a certain symbolism. The city was opening wide to world class commerce. But in neither Norfolk nor Europe did the new techniques of industry arrive much before 1800.

For generations there had been a steady migration of people to Britain's overseas colonies. On the Mayflower in 1620, 64 of the 101 men women and children were from Norfolk. Immigrants gave the name Norwich to many of their settlements, a few they named Norfolk, and they named some after other towns and villages of their old county in England; they became towns and cities in their own right, but still developing while our Norwich was slowly moving toward its more industrial future, and giving up so much of its historic heritage by dismantling its ancient walls, gates and towers.

And yet there are relics for us to hold on to. In the city streets there are still lines of ancient roof-tops and so many churches. Along our river walks there are the Boom Towers, Pull's Ferry (the Watergate), Bishop's Bridge and the Cow Tower. Away from the river, we have all those stretches of ruined city wall.

Beginning at the site of King Street Gate, a full line of the wall leads down to the river, another guards the steep steps of Carrow Hill up to Bracondale. There are important sections of wall at Ber Street, St Stephen's, and St Benedict's Gates. Over the river from there are sections between the Coslany and St Augustine's Gates, more at the gate site at the entrance to Magdalen Street, and finally at Bull Close and River Lane. There are mural towers on Carrow Hill and on Chapelfield and the stub of a tower near the site of the Coslany Gate. Perhaps the most interesting is the many-sided tower on the corner of Bull Close and Silver Road (see page 50). Sections of the city wall and mural towers survived by becoming integral parts of store houses, workshops and dwellings. The Black Tower of Bracondale, our largest mural tower, owes its survival to its use as a snuff mill. Of the gates there is nothing, except that the foundations of many may still be there hidden under modern Tarmac. Of the city ditch, almost all of it is now under houses or 20th century Tarmac. In only one place will you find any sign of it; beside Baker's Road, between St Augustine's Gate and Oak Street. On the south side is a wide grass verge between the road and a length of the city wall. If you stand close to the wall, and look toward Oak Street, toward the site of Coslany Gate (see page 72), you will see that in places the grass under your feet has a shallow depression parallel to the wall; it marks the line of the ditch.

The remains of walls and towers are now legally protected, so that natives of Norwich and the tourists whom we welcome can contemplate and appreciate these relics of our history; it is hoped that descendants of Norwich families from all over the world will come to explore our city and look for signs of the Norwich known to their ancestors. We can only wish that citizens and councils of the late 1700s had found ways to live with at least some of our ancient gates.

Appendix i.   City Gates Dimensions

According to the Norwich City Council Survey Report, 1999 – 2002, about the city walls and gates – for which the first Ordnance Survey map of 1885 and a Kirkpatrick/Ninham etching were helpful references – there is reasonably reliable evidence for the dimensions of King Street Gate. From this, estimates for the dimensions of other city gates became possible. Such features as windows, loops, merlons, coats of arms and archways, and the doors and windows of adjacent buildings were cross-compared, while extant buildings and thoroughfares present in some Henry Ninham sketches and on early Ordnance Survey maps were also studied.

The estimated dimensions tabled on the right may suggest that some standardisation was imposed upon architects and builders, with particular regard to the archways. Each *former* (template) used to construct an arch curvature may have been used for more than one gate; if so, an effective cost saving. Only Brazen Gate is markedly different in its dimensions and proportions, it being one of the last built, and probably having begun as a mural tower. Its dimensions given here are from the 1847 paper by John Britton, as referred to in the Council Survey. For Bishop's Gate, some dimensional information was gained from the surviving Bishopgate Bridge.

After the completion of King Street Gate, building costs may have influenced the dimensions of the gates that followed between 1220 and 1288; but the last two gates, Magdalen and Barre, built in the years 1338-9, reverted to dimensions similar to those of King Street Gate, their size and proportions perhaps reflecting the restricted use experienced at the other gates; also the changing relative importance of the thoroughfares at the time of building.

Name of Gate	Archway		Gatehouse	
	Height to apex	Width	Height to parapet	Width
King Street Gate.	13	12	36	26
Ber Street Gatehouse;	12	9	27	12
Tower;			36	12
Brazen Gate.	12	8.5	28	37
St Stephen's gatehouse;	12	11	28	12
Towers;			36	18
St Giles' Gate;	12	9	32	18
With stairway buttress;				24
St Benedict's Gate.	12	9	31	24
With stairway turret;			37	27
Heigham Gate.	9	7	27	21
After 1742 rebuild;	13	10	24	21
Coslany Gate.	12	8	30	18
St Augustine's Gate.	12	9	30	21
Magdalen Gate.	12	10	32	21
Barre Gate.	13	10	32	18
Bishop's Gate.	12	8	30	18
With stairway turrets;			36	24

(measurements in feet)

City Gates Time Line

Name of gate site	Commonly used names of gate	Year first recorded	Year demolished	Recorded years of repair, after Spynk's work of 1342.
King Street Gate.	Konnigsford, Cunegesford Conisford Gate.	1175	1794	1480: repairs after earthquake. 1664: part of gate fell; repaired. 1793: general repairs.
Ber Street Gate.	Berg Gate, Bear Street gate.	1220	1808	c.1450: damaged 'low' tower removed? 1558: repairs. 1727: city side rebuilt in brick, turret added to remaining round tower.
Brazen Gate.	St Winnold's Gate, Swine Gate, New Gate, Iron Gate, Brazen Doors.	1285	1792	1726: archway enlarged.
St Stephen's Gate.	Nedeham Gate.	1285	1793	c.1720: 1757. 1761, roof tiled.
St Giles' Gate.	Newport Gate.	1288	1792	1756: repairs to roof. 1763: general repairs.
St Benedict's Gate.	Westwick Gate.	1288	1793	1451 and 1481: repairs to gate and wall, and again in 1679. c.1720: stair turret enclosed. Last remnant of gate lost in WWII.
Heigham Gate.	Hell Gate, Black Gate.	1221	c.1800	1742: rebuilt, archway enlarged, and roof added after removal of battlements.
St Martin's at Oak.	Coslany (Cos'n'y) Gate.	1275	1808	1680 and 1699. 1760: brick rebuild?
St Augustine's Gate.	St Austin's Gate.	1225	1794	1338–1343 and 1676, general repairs.
Magdalen Gate.	Fyebrigge Gate, Lepers' Gate.	1339	1808	1549: rebel damage 'made new.' 1756: front rebuilt.
Pockthorpe Gate.	Barre Gate.	1338?	1792	1549: rebel damage 'made new.' 1757: battlements repaired. 1790: chimney added
Bishop's Gate.		1332	1791	1467: general repairs. 1549 – rebel damage repaired.

Trades in the gate streets in the late 1700s

	Building trades	Wood work	Metal work	Passenger and mail carriers	Coach and cart builders	Coal	Beer and wine	Inns and pubs	Butchers	Bakers and millers	Fashion and fabrics	Boots and shoe trades
King Street	7	2	1	1	3	7	6	20+		8	12	1
Ber Street	2	3	1	1			1	11	16	4	1	2
All Saints' Green to Brazen Gate.	2							1				
St Stephen's Street	4	3	1		3			10		4	11	2
St Giles' Street	3		1	2	6		3	4		1	5	1
Bethel Street	3			1			1	2		1	4	
St Benedict's.	4		1	1	2		3	9		4	10	
Westwick Street to Heigham Gate	2		2			1					10	1
Coslany Street	2	1	1	2	4	1	5	4	2	5	18	3
St Augustine's	1						1	6		2	3	
Magdalen Street	3	3	4		8		5	9+		5	20+	6
Barrack Street							6	15+				
Bishopgate Street	1		1	1			1	3				1

Metal work: blacksmiths, whitesmiths (metal plating and finishing), coppersmiths and braziers.
Fashion: clothiers, drapers, silk workers, hair dressers and wig makers.
Also in King Street: 8 premises to do with shipping and staithes.

The numbers for each trade varied throughout this period.

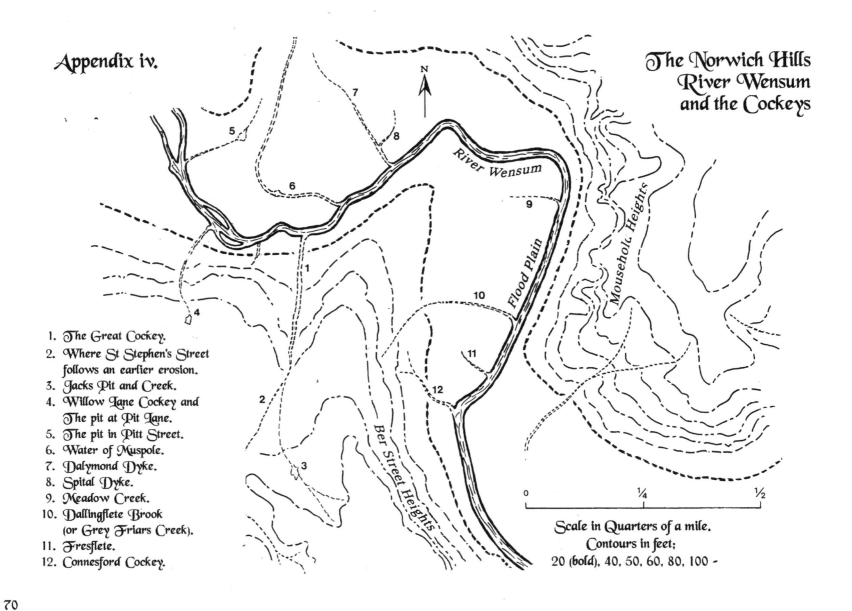

Appendix iv.

The Norwich Hills
River Wensum
and the Cockeys

N

River Wensum

Mouseholt Heights

Flood Plain

Ber Street Heights

1. The Great Cockey.
2. Where St Stephen's Street
   follows an earlier erosion.
3. Jacks Pit and Creek.
4. Willow Lane Cockey and
   The pit at Pit Lane.
5. The pit in Pitt Street.
6. Water of Muspole.
7. Dalymond Dyke.
8. Spital Dyke.
9. Meadow Creek.
10. Dallingflete Brook
    (or Grey Friars Creek).
11. Fresflete.
12. Connesford Cockey.

0   ¼   ½

Scale in Quarters of a mile.
Contours in feet;
20 (bold), 40, 50, 60, 80, 100 -

References

VIEWS OF THE GATES OF NORWICH. Robert Fitch. Cundall, 1861. *Historical introduction by Robert Fitch, drawings / etchings by John Kirkpatrick / John Ninham.*

ILLUSTRATIONS BY HENRY NINHAM; *originals held by Norfolk Museums and Archaeology Service.*

EAST ELEVATION OF NORWICH CASTLE; William Wilkins. *Norfolk Museums and Archaeology Service.*

THE WALLS OF NORWICH; The report to Norwich City Council Committee. Jarrold and Sons, 1910.

NORWICH CITY WALLS SURVEY; Norwich City council, 1999 – 2002.

RECORDS OF THE CITY OF NORWICH vol. 2; Hudson, W. and Tingey, J.C., Jarrold and Sons, 1910.

CHASE'S NORWICH DIRECTORY; W. Chase and Co., 1783; *Plan of the City of Norwich.*

NORFOLK & NORWICH MAPS AND PLANS; Norwich Plans, 1541 – 1914; Geo. A. Stephen F.L.A., Jarrold and Sons, 1928. *T. Kirkpatrick's North East Prospect, 1723; Corbridge's Plan, 1727.*

THE HISTORY OF THE CITY OF NORWICH; Francis Blomefield, 1806 edition.

THE COMMOYSON IN NORFOLK, 1549; Nicholas Sotherton. Larks Press.

A JOURNAL OF THE PLAGUE YEAR; Daniel Defoe. Penguin Classics 1995.

IF STONES COULD SPEAK; R. H. Mottram. Museum Press, 1955.

NORWICH – THE GROWTH OF A CITY; The Norwich Museums Committee, 1963.

NORWICH; Sylvia Haymon. Longman Young Books, 1973.

DISAPPEARING NORWICH; George A. F. Plunkett. Terence Dalton Limited, 1988.

A HISTORY OF NORWICH; Frank Meeres. Phillimore & Co. Ltd, 1998. *Front end paper, Perspective map by Cuningham, 1558; rear end paper, Hochstetter's Plan, 1789; page 71, Cleer / Kirkpatrick map, 1696.*

A PROSPECT OF NORWICH; George Nobbs. Prospect Press, 2003.

FIRST EDITION ORDNANCE SURVEY MAPS, 1:1250 scale, 1884, 1885, 1886; *Norfolk and Norwich Heritage Centre, Norfolk Library and Information Service, The Forum, Norwich.*

MEDIEVAL BUILDING TECHNIQUES, G. Binding. (Translation, A Cameron.) Tempus Publishing Limited, 2004.

Acknowledgements

For finding documents, plans and old preserved books, I owe my gratitude to
the staff of the Norfolk Record Office, Norfolk Museums and Archaeology Service,
Norfolk Library and Information Service, and Norwich City Council Planning Department.

For their help and advice I am particularly grateful to:
Trevor Heaton, Features Editor at Archant Newspapers, Norwich,
for suggesting this book, and Derek James, their Features Writer,
for his glowing Foreword.
Also Mike Loveday, Chief Executive of Norwich Heart;
Kate Knights, Conservation and Design officer, Norwich City Council;
Mike Bennett of the Richard III Museum, York, and
Jane Apps, Head Steward of Hever Castle, Kent.

Special thanks to
Susan Yaxley of Larks Press,
for her thorough and
insightful editing;
my good friend Natalie
and my son Leon
for their technical support;

and most especially
my wife Ann,
for all her help and
patience.